NIST Special Publication 800-83

Guide to Malware Incident Prevention and Handling

Recommendations of the National Institute of Standards and Technology

Peter Mell
Karen Kent
Joseph Nusbaum

COMPUTER SECURITY

Computer Security Division
Information Technology Laboratory
National Institute of Standards and Technology
Gaithersburg, MD 20899-8930

November 2005

U.S. Department of Commerce

Carlos M. Gutierrez, Secretary

Technology Administration

Michelle O'Neill, Acting Under Secretary of
Commerce for Technology

National Institute of Standards and Technology

William A. Jeffrey, Director

Acknowledgments

The authors, Peter Mell of the National Institute of Standards and Technology (NIST) and Karen Kent and Joseph Nusbaum of Booz Allen Hamilton, wish to thank their colleagues who reviewed drafts of this document and contributed to its technical content. The authors would particularly like to acknowledge Tim Grance and Murugiah Souppaya of NIST and Lucinda Gagliano, Thomas Goff, and Pius Uzamere of Booz Allen Hamilton for their keen and insightful assistance throughout the development of the document. The authors would also like to express their thanks to security experts Mike Danseglio (Microsoft), Kurt Dillard (Microsoft), Michael Gerdes (Getronics RedSiren Security Solutions), Peter Szor (Symantec), Miles Tracy (U.S. Federal Reserve System), and Lenny Zeltser (Gemini Systems LLC), as well as representatives from the General Accounting Office, and for their particularly valuable comments and suggestions.

The National Institute of Standards and Technology would also like to express its appreciation and thanks to the Department of Homeland Security for its sponsorship and support of NIST Special Publication 800-83.

Trademark Information

All product names are registered trademarks or trademarks of their respective companies.

Table of Contents

List of Appendices

List of Figures

List of Tables

Executive Summary

Malware, also known as malicious code and malicious software, refers to a program that is inserted into a system, usually covertly, with the intent of compromising the confidentiality, integrity, or availability of the victim's data, applications, or operating system or otherwise annoying or disrupting the victim. Malware has become the most significant external threat to most systems, causing widespread damage and disruption, and necessitating extensive recovery efforts within most organizations. Spyware— malware intended to violate a user's privacy—has also become a major concern to organizations. Although privacy-violating malware has been in use for many years, it has become much more widespread recently, with spyware invading many systems to monitor personal activities and conduct financial fraud. Organizations also face similar threats from a few forms of non-malware threats that are often associated with malware. One of these forms that has become commonplace is phishing, which is using deceptive computer-based means to trick individuals into disclosing sensitive information. Another common form is virus hoaxes, which are false warnings of new malware threats.

This publication provides recommendations for improving an organization's malware incident prevention measures. It also gives extensive recommendations for enhancing an organization's existing incident response capability so that it is better prepared to handle malware incidents, particularly widespread ones. The recommendations address several major forms of malware, including viruses, worms, Trojan horses, malicious mobile code, blended attacks, spyware tracking cookies, and attacker tools such as backdoors and rootkits. The recommendations encompass various transmission mechanisms, including network services (e.g., e-mail, Web browsing, file sharing) and removable media.

Implementing the following recommendations should facilitate more efficient and effective malware incident response activities for Federal departments and agencies.

Organizations should develop and implement an approach to malware incident prevention.

Organizations should plan and implement an approach to malware incident prevention based on the attack vectors that are most likely to be used, both currently and in the near future. Because the effectiveness of prevention techniques may vary depending on the environment (i.e., a technique that works well in a managed environment might be ineffective in a non-managed environment), organizations should choose preventive methods that are well-suited to their environment and systems. An organization's approach to malware incident prevention should incorporate policy considerations, awareness programs for users and information technology (IT) staff, and vulnerability and threat mitigation efforts.

Organizations should ensure that their policies support the prevention of malware incidents.

An organization's policy statements should be used as the basis for additional malware prevention efforts, such as user and IT staff awareness, vulnerability mitigation, and security tool deployment and configuration. If an organization does not state malware prevention considerations clearly in its policy, it is unlikely to perform malware prevention activities consistently and effectively. Malware prevention– related policy should be as general as possible to allow flexibility in policy implementation and to reduce the need for frequent policy updates, but should also be specific enough to make the intent and scope of the policy clear. Malware prevention–related policy should include provisions related to remote workers—both those using systems controlled by the organization and those using systems outside of the organization's control (e.g., contractor computers, employees' home computers, business partners' computers, mobile devices).

Organizations should incorporate malware incident prevention and handling into their awareness programs.

Organizations should implement awareness programs that include guidance to users on malware incident prevention. All users should be made aware of the ways that malware spreads, the risks that malware poses, the inability of technical controls to prevent all incidents, and the importance of users in preventing incidents. Awareness programs should also make users aware of the policy and procedures that apply to malware incident handling, such as how to detect malware on a computer, how to report suspected infections, and what users might need to do to assist incident handlers. In addition, the organization should conduct awareness activities for IT staff involved in malware incident prevention and provide training on specific tasks.

Organizations should have vulnerability mitigation capabilities to help prevent malware incidents.

Organizations should have documented policy, processes, and procedures to mitigate operating system and application vulnerabilities that malware might exploit. Because a vulnerability usually can be mitigated through one or more methods, organizations should use an appropriate combination of techniques, including patch management, application of security configuration guides and checklists, and additional host hardening measures so that effective techniques are readily available for various types of vulnerabilities.

Organizations should have threat mitigation capabilities to assist in containing malware incidents.

Organizations should perform threat mitigation efforts to detect and stop malware before it can affect its targets. The most commonly used threat mitigation technical control is antivirus software; NIST strongly recommends that organizations deploy antivirus software on all systems for which satisfactory antivirus software is available. To mitigate spyware threats, either antivirus software with the ability to recognize spyware threats or specialized spyware detection and removal utilities should be used on all systems for which satisfactory software is available. Additional technical controls that are helpful for malware threat mitigation include intrusion prevention systems, firewalls, routers, and certain application configuration settings. The System and Information Integrity family of security controls in NIST Special Publication 800-53, *Recommended Security Controls for Federal Information Systems*, recommends having malware and spyware protection mechanisms on various types of hosts, including workstations, servers, mobile computing devices, firewalls, e-mail servers, and remote access servers.

Organizations should have a robust incident response process capability that addresses malware incident handling.

As defined in NIST Special Publication 800-61, *Computer Security Incident Handling Guide*, the incident response process has four main phases: preparation, detection and analysis, containment/eradication/recovery, and post-incident activity. Some major recommendations for malware incident handling, by phase or subphase, are as follows:

- **Preparation.** Organizations should perform preparatory measures to ensure that they can respond effectively to malware incidents. Recommended actions include—

  - Developing malware-specific incident handling policies and procedures

  - Regularly conducting malware-oriented training and exercises

  - Designating a few individuals or a small team, in advance, to be responsible for coordinating the organization's responses to malware incidents

- Establishing several communication mechanisms so that coordination among incident handlers, technical staff, management, and users can be sustained during adverse events.

■ **Detection and Analysis.** Organizations should strive to detect and validate malware incidents rapidly because infections can spread through an organization within a matter of minutes. Early detection can help an organization minimize the number of infected systems, which will lessen the magnitude of the recovery effort and the amount of damage the organization sustains. Recommended actions include—

- Monitoring malware advisories and alerts produced by technical controls (e.g., antivirus software, spyware detection and removal utilities, intrusion detection systems) to identify likely impending malware incidents. Such monitoring gives organizations the opportunity to prevent incidents by altering their security posture.

- Reviewing malware incident data from such primary sources as user reports, IT staff reports, and technical controls to identify malware-related activity.

- Constructing trusted toolkits on removable media that contain up-to-date tools for identifying malware, listing currently running processes, and performing other analysis actions.

- Establishing a set of prioritization criteria that identify the appropriate level of response for various malware-related incidents.

■ **Containment.** Malware incident containment has two major components: stopping the spread of malware and preventing further damage to systems. Nearly every malware incident requires containment actions. In addressing an incident, it is important for an organization to decide which methods of containment to employ early in the response. Organizations should have strategies and procedures in place for making containment-related decisions that reflect the level of risk acceptable to the organization. Containment strategies should support incident handlers in selecting the appropriate combination of containment methods for a particular situation. Organizational policies should clearly state who has the authority to make major containment decisions and under what circumstances various actions are appropriate. Specific containment-related recommendations include the following:

- It can be helpful to provide users with instructions on how to identify infections and what measures to take if a system is infected; however, organizations should not rely primarily on users for containing malware incidents.

- If malware cannot be identified and contained by updated antivirus software, organizations should be prepared to use other security tools to contain it. Organizations should also be prepared to submit copies of unknown malware to their security software vendors for analysis, as well as contacting trusted parties such as incident response organizations and antivirus vendors when guidance is needed on handling new threats.

- Organizations should be prepared to shut down or block services such as e-mail used by malware to contain an incident and should understand the consequences of doing so. Organizations should also be prepared to respond to problems caused by other organizations disabling their own services in response to a malware incident.

- Organizations should be prepared to place additional temporary restrictions on network connectivity to contain a malware incident, such as suspending Internet access or physically disconnecting systems from networks, recognizing the impact that the restrictions might have on organizational functions.

Identifying those hosts infected by malware is another vital step in containing many malware incidents, particularly widespread ones. Identifying infected hosts is often complicated by the dynamic nature of computing (e.g., remote access, mobile users). Organizations should carefully consider host identification issues before a large-scale malware incident occurs so that they are prepared to use multiple strategies for identifying infected hosts as part of their containment efforts. Organizations should select a sufficiently broad range of identification approaches and should develop procedures and technical capabilities to perform each selected approach effectively when a major malware incident occurs.

■ **Eradication.** The primary goal of eradication is to remove malware from infected systems. Because of the potential need for extensive eradication efforts, organizations should be prepared to use various combinations of eradication techniques simultaneously for different situations. Organizations should also consider performing awareness activities that set expectations for eradication and recovery efforts; these activities can be helpful in reducing the stress that major malware incidents can cause.

■ **Recovery.** The two main aspects of recovery from malware incidents are restoring the functionality and data of infected systems and lifting temporary containment measures. Organizations should carefully consider possible worst-case scenarios and determine how recovery should be performed, including rebuilding compromised systems from scratch or known good backups. Determining when to remove temporary containment measures, such as suspension of services or connectivity, is often a difficult decision during major malware incidents. Incident response teams should strive to keep containment measures in place until the estimated number of infected systems and systems vulnerable to infection is sufficiently low that subsequent incidents should be of little consequence. However, even though the incident response team should assess the risks of restoring services or connectivity, management ultimately should be responsible for determining what should be done based on the incident response team's recommendations and management's understanding of the business impact of maintaining the containment measures.

■ **Post-Incident Activity.** Because the handling of malware incidents can be extremely expensive, it is particularly important for organizations to conduct a robust assessment of lessons learned after major malware incidents to prevent similar incidents from occurring. Capturing the lessons learned from the handling of such incidents should help an organization improve its incident handling capability and malware defenses, including identifying needed changes to security policy, software configurations, and malware detection and prevention software deployments.

Organizations should establish malware incident prevention and handling capabilities that address current and short-term future threats.

Because new malware threats arise constantly, organizations should establish malware incident prevention and handling capabilities that are robust and flexible enough to address both current and short-term future threats and that can be modified and built on to address long-term future threats. Both malware and the defenses against malware continue to evolve, each in response to improvements in the other. For this reason, organizations should stay up-to-date on the latest types of threats and the security controls available to combat each type. As a new category of threats becomes more serious, organizations should plan and implement appropriate controls to mitigate it. Awareness of new and emerging threats and protective capabilities should be part of every organization's efforts to prevent malware incidents.

1. Introduction

1.1 Authority

The National Institute of Standards and Technology (NIST) developed this document in furtherance of its statutory responsibilities under the Federal Information Security Management Act (FISMA) of 2002, Public Law 107-347.

NIST is responsible for developing standards and guidelines, including minimum requirements, for providing adequate information security for all agency operations and assets; but such standards and guidelines shall not apply to national security systems. This guideline is consistent with the requirements of the Office of Management and Budget (OMB) Circular A-130, Section 8b(3), "Securing Agency Information Systems," as analyzed in A-130, Appendix IV: Analysis of Key Sections. Supplemental information is provided in A-130, Appendix III.

This guideline has been prepared for use by Federal agencies. It may be used by nongovernmental organizations on a voluntary basis and is not subject to copyright, though attribution is desired.

Nothing in this document should be taken to contradict standards and guidelines made mandatory and binding on Federal agencies by the Secretary of Commerce under statutory authority, nor should these guidelines be interpreted as altering or superseding the existing authorities of the Secretary of Commerce, Director of the OMB, or any other Federal official.

1.2 Purpose and Scope

This publication is intended to help organizations understand the threats posed by malware and mitigate the risks associated with malware incidents. In addition to providing background information on the major categories of malware, it provides practical, real-world guidance on preventing malware incidents and responding to malware incidents in an effective, efficient manner.

1.3 Audience

This document has been created for computer security staff and program managers, technical support staff and managers, computer security incident response teams, and system and network administrators, who are responsible for preventing, preparing for, or responding to malware incidents. Portions of the guide are also intended for end users who seek a better understanding of malware threats and the actions they can take to prevent incidents and respond to incidents more effectively.

1.4 Document Structure

The remainder of this guide is divided into four major sections. Section 2 defines, discusses, and compares the various categories of malware. Section 3 provides recommendations for preventing malware incidents through several layers of controls. Section 4 explains the malware incident response process, focusing on practical strategies for detection, containment, eradication, and recovery in managed and non-managed environments. Likely future developments and trends in malware are highlighted in Section 5.

The guide also contains several appendices with supporting material. Appendix A presents a summary of the incident prevention and containment technologies discussed throughout the document, as well as general guidance on the effectiveness of each technology in different environments and circumstances. Appendix B presents simple malware handling scenarios that could be used as a basis for team discussions and exercises. Appendices C and D contain a glossary and an acronym list, respectively. Appendix E lists print resources, and Appendix F identifies online resources, that can help readers gain a better understanding of malware, malware incident prevention, and malware incident handling. Appendix G contains an index.

2. Malware Categories

Malware, also known as *malicious code* and *malicious software*,[1] refers to a program that is inserted into a system, usually covertly, with the intent of compromising the confidentiality, integrity, or availability of the victim's data, applications, or operating system (OS) or of otherwise annoying or disrupting the victim. Malware such as viruses and worms is usually designed to perform these nefarious functions in such a way that users are unaware of them, at least initially. In the 1980s, malware was occasionally a nuisance or inconvenience to individuals and organizations; today, malware is the most significant external threat to most systems, causing widespread damage and disruption and necessitating extensive recovery efforts within most organizations. *Spyware*—malware intended to violate a user's privacy—has also become a major concern to organizations. Although privacy-violating malware has been in use for many years, its use became much more widespread in 2003 and 2004, with spyware invading many systems to monitor personal activities and conduct financial fraud.

As a foundation for later sections, this section provides an overview of the various categories of malware, which include viruses, worms, Trojan horses, and malicious mobile code, as well as combinations of these, known as blended attacks.[2] Malware also includes attacker tools such as backdoors, rootkits, and keystroke loggers, and tracking cookies used as spyware. The discussion of each category explains how the malware typically enters and infects systems and spreads; how it works (in general terms); what its objectives are; and how it affects systems. The section also provides a brief discussion of a few threats that are not malware, but are often discussed in conjunction with malware. The section also presents a brief history of malware to indicate the relative importance of each malware category in the past and the present. The section concludes by comparing the categories of malware to identify similarities and differences.

2.1 Viruses

A *virus* is designed to self-replicate—make copies of itself—and distribute the copies to other files, programs, or computers. Each virus has an infection mechanism; for example, viruses can insert themselves into host programs or data files (i.e., malicious macro code within a word processing file). The virus *payload* contains the code for the virus's objective, which can range from the relatively benign (e.g., annoying people, stating personal opinions) to the extremely malicious (e.g., forwarding personal information to others, wiping out systems). Many viruses also have a *trigger*—a condition that causes the payload to be executed, which usually involves user interaction (e.g., opening a file, running a program, clicking on an e-mail file attachment). The two major types of viruses are *compiled viruses*, which are executed by an operating system (OS), and *interpreted viruses*, which are executed by an application. This section discusses both types of viruses, as well as the various obfuscation techniques that viruses use to avoid detection.

2.1.1 Compiled Viruses

A *compiled virus* is a virus that has had its source code converted by a compiler program into a format that can be directly executed by an OS. Compiled viruses typically fall into three categories:

- **File Infector.** A *file infector virus* attaches itself to executable programs, such as word processors, spreadsheet applications, and computer games. When the virus has infected a

---

[1] The word *malware* is a shortened form of the term *malicious software*.

[2] There is not consensus in the security community on the precise differences between certain categories of malware. The definitions presented in this guide are based on the generally accepted characteristics of each malware category.

program, it propagates to infect other programs on the system, as well as other systems that use a shared infected program. Jerusalem and Cascade are two of the best known file infector viruses.[3]

■ **Boot Sector.** A *boot sector virus* infects the master boot record (MBR) of a hard drive or the boot sector of a hard drive or removable media, such as floppy diskettes. The boot sector is an area at the beginning of a drive or disk where information about the drive or disk structure is stored. Boot sectors contain boot programs that are run at host startup to boot the OS. The MBR of a hard drive is a unique location on the disk where a computer's basic input/output system (BIOS) can locate and load the boot program. Removable media, such as floppy disks, need not be bootable to infect the system; if an infected disk is in the drive when the computer boots, the virus could be executed. Boot sector viruses are easily concealed, have a high rate of success, and can harm a computer to the point of making it completely inoperable. Symptoms of boot sector virus infection on a computer include an error message during booting or the inability to boot. Form, Michelangelo, and Stoned are examples of boot sector viruses.

■ **Multipartite.** A *multipartite virus* uses multiple infection methods, typically infecting both files and boot sectors. Accordingly, multipartite viruses combine the characteristics of file infector and boot sector viruses. Examples of multipartite viruses include Flip and Invader.

In addition to infecting files, compiled viruses can reside in the memory of infected systems so that each time a new program is executed, the virus infects the program. Among compiled viruses, boot sector viruses are the most likely to be *memory resident*. Viruses that are memory resident stay in memory for an extended period of time and therefore are likely to infect more files and to interfere more frequently with normal system operations than non-memory-resident viruses.

2.1.2 Interpreted Viruses

Unlike compiled viruses, which can be executed by an OS, *interpreted viruses* are composed of source code that can be executed only by a particular application or service. Interpreted viruses have become very common because they are much easier to write and modify than other types of viruses. A relatively unskilled attacker can acquire an interpreted virus, review and modify its source code, and distribute it to others. There are often dozens of variants of a single interpreted virus, most with only trivial changes from the original. The two major types of interpreted viruses are macro viruses and scripting viruses.

Macro viruses are the most prevalent and successful type of virus. These viruses attach themselves to application documents, such as word processing files and spreadsheets, and use the application's macro programming language to execute and propagate. Macro viruses use the macro programming capabilities that many popular software packages, such as Microsoft Office, use to automate complex or repetitive tasks. These viruses tend to spread quickly because users frequently share documents from applications with macro capabilities. In addition, when a macro virus infection occurs, the virus infects the template that the program uses to create and open files. Once a template is infected, every document that is created or opened with that template is also infected. The Concept, Marker, and Melissa viruses are well-known examples of macro viruses.

Scripting viruses are very similar to macro viruses. The primary difference is that a macro virus is written in a language understood by a particular application, such as a word processor, whereas a scripting virus is written in a language understood by a service run by the OS. For example, the Windows Scripting Host

---

[3] For more information on these examples, as well as the other examples cited throughout this section, visit the virus information Web sites listed in the Technical Resource Sites section of Appendix F. The compiled virus examples listed in this section are mostly from the early 1990's, when they were the most common form of malware.

feature on some Microsoft Windows systems can execute scripts written in VBScript. Examples of well-known scripting viruses are First and Love Stages.

2.1.3 Virus Obfuscation Techniques

Most viruses are created using one or more *obfuscation techniques*—ways of constructing a virus that make it more difficult to detect. If a virus is hard to detect, it is likely to spread more widely. The following are commonly used obfuscation techniques:[4]

- **Self-Encryption and Self-Decryption.** Some viruses can encrypt and decrypt their virus code bodies, concealing them from direct examination. Viruses that employ encryption might use multiple layers of encryption or random cryptographic keys, which make each instance of the virus appear to be different, even though the underlying code is the same.

- **Polymorphism.** Polymorphism is a particularly robust form of self-encryption. A polymorphic virus generally makes several changes to the default encryption settings, as well as altering the decryption code. In a polymorphic virus, the content of the underlying virus code body does not change; encryption alters its appearance only.

- **Metamorphism.** The idea behind metamorphism is to alter the content of the virus itself, rather than hiding the content with encryption. The virus can be altered in several ways—for example, by adding unneeded code sequences to the source code or changing the sequence of pieces of the source code. The altered code is then recompiled to create a virus executable that looks fundamentally different from the original.

- **Stealth.** A stealth virus uses various techniques to conceal the characteristics of an infection. For example, many stealth viruses interfere with OS file listings so that the reported file sizes reflect the original values and do not include the size of the virus added to each infected file.

- **Armoring.** The intent of armoring is to write a virus so that it attempts to prevent antivirus software or human experts from analyzing the virus's functions through disassembly, traces, and other means.

- **Tunneling.** A virus that employs tunneling inserts itself into a low level of the OS so that it can intercept low-level OS calls. By placing itself below the antivirus software, the virus attempts to manipulate the OS to prevent detection by antivirus software.

Antivirus software vendors design their products to attempt to compensate for the use of any combination of obfuscation techniques. Older obfuscation techniques, including self-encryption, polymorphism, and stealth, are generally handled effectively by antivirus software. However, newer, more complex obfuscation techniques, such as metamorphism, are still emerging and can be considerably more difficult for antivirus software to overcome.

2.2 Worms

Worms are self-replicating programs that are completely self-contained, meaning that they do not require a host program to infect a victim. Worms also are self-propagating; unlike viruses, they can create fully functional copies and execute themselves without user intervention. This has made worms increasingly popular with attackers, because a worm has the potential to infect many more systems in a short period of time than a virus can. Worms take advantage of known vulnerabilities and configuration weaknesses,

---

[4]   For a more comprehensive list of virus obfuscation techniques, consult *The Art of Computer Virus Research and Defense* by Peter Szor (Addison-Wesley, 2005).

such as unsecured Windows shares. Although some worms are intended mainly to waste system and network resources, many worms damage systems by installing backdoors (discussed in Section 2.7.1), perform distributed denial of service (DDoS) attacks against other hosts, or perform other malicious acts. The two primary categories of worms are network service worms and mass mailing worms.

Network service worms spread by exploiting a vulnerability in a network service associated with an OS or an application. Once a worm infects a system, it typically uses that system to scan for other systems running the targeted service and then attempts to infect those systems as well. Because they act completely without human intervention, network service worms can typically propagate more quickly than other forms of malware. The rapid spread of worms and the intensive scanning they often perform to identify new targets often overwhelm networks and security systems (e.g., network intrusion detection sensors), as well as infected systems. Examples of network service worms are Sasser and Witty.

Mass mailing worms are similar to e-mail–borne viruses, with the primary difference being that mass mailing worms are self-contained instead of infecting an existing file as e-mail–borne viruses do. Once a mass mailing worm has infected a system, it typically searches the system for e-mail addresses and then sends copies of itself to those addresses, using either the system's e-mail client or a self-contained mailer built into the worm itself. A mass mailing worm typically sends a single copy of itself to multiple recipients at once. Besides overwhelming e-mail servers and networks with massive volumes of e-mails, mass mailing worms often cause serious performance issues for infected systems. Examples of mass mailing worms are Beagle, Mydoom, and Netsky.

2.3   Trojan Horses

Named after the wooden horse from Greek mythology, *Trojan horses* are non-replicating programs that appear to be benign but actually have a hidden malicious purpose.[5] Some Trojan horses are intended to replace existing files, such as system and application executables, with malicious versions; others add another application to systems instead of overwriting existing files. Trojan horses tend to conform to any of the following three models:

- Continuing to perform the function of the original program and also performing separate, unrelated malicious activity (e.g., a game that also collects application passwords)

- Continuing to perform the function of the original program but modifying the function to perform malicious activity (e.g., a Trojan horse version of a login program that collects passwords) or to disguise other malicious activity (e.g., a Trojan horse version of a process-listing program that does not display other malicious processes)

- Performing a malicious function that completely replaces the function of the original program (e.g., a file that claims to be a game but actually just deletes all system files when it is run).

Trojan horses can be difficult to detect. Because many are specifically designed to conceal their presence on systems and perform the original program's function properly, users and system administrators may not notice them. Many newer Trojan horses also make use of some of the same obfuscation techniques that viruses use to avoid detection.

The use of Trojan horses to distribute spyware programs has become increasingly common. Spyware is often bundled with software, such as certain peer-to-peer file sharing client programs; when the user installs the supposedly benign software, it then covertly installs spyware programs. Trojan horses also often deliver other types of attacker tools onto systems, which can provide unauthorized access to or

---

[5]   Trojan horses are sometimes referred to as *Trojans*.

usage of infected systems. These tools may be bundled with the Trojan horse or downloaded by the Trojan horse after it is placed onto a system and run. Section 2.7 describes several types of malicious tools that are commonly delivered by means of Trojan horses.

Trojan horses can cause serious technical issues on systems. For example, a Trojan horse that replaces legitimate system executables may cause certain functionality to be performed incorrectly or lost altogether. Spyware-related Trojan horses have been particularly disruptive to many systems because they are often intentionally invasive, making many modifications to systems and deploying themselves so that their removal causes serious disruption to the system, in some cases to the point where the system can no longer function. Trojan horses and the tools they install can also be resource-intensive, causing noticeable performance degradation on infected systems. Some well-known Trojan horses are SubSeven, Back Orifice, and Optix Pro.

2.4 Malicious Mobile Code

Mobile code is software that is transmitted from a remote system to be executed on a local system, typically without the user's explicit instruction.[6] It has become a popular way of writing programs that can be used by many different operating systems and applications, such as Web browsers and e-mail clients. Although mobile code is typically benign, attackers have learned that malicious mobile code can be an effective way of attacking systems, as well as a good mechanism for transmitting viruses, worms, and Trojan horses to users' workstations. Malicious mobile code differs significantly from viruses and worms in that it does not infect files or attempt to propagate itself. Instead of exploiting particular vulnerabilities, it often affects systems by taking advantage of the default privileges granted to mobile code. Popular languages for malicious mobile code include Java, ActiveX, JavaScript, and VBScript. One of the best-known examples of malicious mobile code is Nimda, which used JavaScript. Section 2.5 contains additional information on Nimda.

2.5 Blended Attacks

A *blended attack* is an instance of malware that uses multiple infection or transmission methods. The well-known Nimda "worm" is actually an example of a blended attack.[7] It used four distribution methods:

- **E-mail.** When a user on a vulnerable host opened an infected e-mail attachment, Nimda exploited a vulnerability in the Web browser used to display HTML-based e-mail. After infecting the host, Nimda then looked for e-mail addresses on the host and then sent copies of itself to those addresses.

- **Windows Shares.** Nimda scanned hosts for unsecured Windows file shares; it then used NetBIOS as a transport mechanism to infect files on that host. If a user ran an infected file, this would activate Nimda on that host.

- **Web Servers.** Nimda scanned Web servers, looking for known vulnerabilities in Microsoft Internet Information Services (IIS). If it found a vulnerable server, it attempted to transfer a copy of itself to the server and to infect the server and its files.

---

[6] For more information on mobile code, read NIST Special Publication (SP) 800-28, *Guidelines on Active Content and Mobile Code*, available from the Computer Security Resource Center (CSRC) Web site at http://csrc.nist.gov/publications/nistpubs/.
[7] More information on Nimda is available from *CERT®/CC Advisory CA-2001-26 Nimda Worm*, available at http://www.cert.org/advisories/CA-2001-26.html.

■ **Web Clients.** If a vulnerable Web client visited a Web server that had been infected by Nimda, the client's workstation would become infected.

In addition to using the methods described above, blended attacks can spread through such services as instant messaging and peer-to-peer file sharing. Many instances of blended attacks, like Nimda, are incorrectly referred to as worms because they have some worm characteristics. In fact, Nimda has characteristics of viruses, worms, and malicious mobile code. Another example of a blended attack is Bugbear, which acted as both a mass mailing worm and a network service worm. Because blended attacks are more complex than single-method malware, they are considerably harder to create.

Blended attacks do not have to use multiple methods simultaneously to spread; they can also perform multiple infections in sequence. This is becoming more popular, primarily as a way of delivering and installing Trojan horses on systems. For example, a virus, a worm, or malicious mobile code that successfully enters a system can install and run a copy of a Trojan horse. The Trojan horse can then perform additional malicious acts, such as installing spyware on the system.

2.6 Tracking Cookies

A *cookie* is a small data file that holds information about the use of a particular Web site.[8] *Session cookies* are temporary cookies that are valid only for a single Web site session. *Persistent cookies* are stored on a computer indefinitely so that the site can identify the user during subsequent visits. The intended use of a persistent cookie is to record user preferences for a single Web site so that the site can automatically customize its appearance or behavior for the user's future visits. In this way, persistent cookies can help Web sites serve their users more effectively.

Unfortunately, persistent cookies also can be misused as spyware to track a user's Web browsing activities for questionable reasons without the user's knowledge or consent. For example, a marketing firm could place advertisements on many Web sites and use a single cookie on a user's machine to track the user's activity on all of those Web sites, creating a detailed profile of the user's behavior. Cookies used in this way are known as *tracking cookies*. Information collected by tracking cookies is often sold to other parties and used to target advertisements and other directed content at the user. Most spyware detection and removal utilities specifically look for tracking cookies on systems.

Another way to capture and deliver a user's private information is through the use of Web bugs. A *Web bug* is a tiny graphic on a Web site that is referenced within the Hypertext Markup Language (HTML) content of a Web page or e-mail. The graphic has no purpose other than to collect information about the user viewing the HTML content. Web bugs are usually invisible to users because they typically consist of only 1 pixel. Like tracking cookies, Web bugs are often used by marketing firms. They can collect information such as the user's Internet Protocol (IP) address and Web browser type and can also access a tracking cookie. These actions enable Web bugs to be used as spyware to create personal profiles of individual users.

2.7 Attacker Tools

As part of a malware infection or other system compromise, various types of attacker tools might be delivered to a system. These tools, which are forms of malware, allow attackers to have unauthorized access to or use of infected systems and their data, or to launch additional attacks. When transferred by other malware, attacker tools can be delivered as part of the malware itself, (e.g., in a Trojan horse) or delivered after an infection occurs. For example, a worm-infected system might be directed by the worm

---

[8]   Cookies often store data in plaintext, which could allow an unauthorized party that accesses a cookie to use or alter the data stored in it. Some Web sites create encrypted cookies, which protect the data from unauthorized access.

to contact a particular malicious Web site, download tools from that site, and install them on the system. Sections 2.7.1 through 2.7.6 describe several popular types of attacker tools.

2.7.1 Backdoors

Backdoor is a general term for a malicious program that listens for commands on a certain Transmission Control Protocol (TCP) or User Datagram Protocol (UDP) port. Most backdoors consist of a client component and a server component. The client resides on the intruder's remote computer, and the server resides on the infected system. When a connection between client and server is established, the remote intruder has some degree of control over the infected computer. At a minimum, most backdoors allow an attacker to perform a certain set of actions on a system, such as transferring files, acquiring passwords, or executing arbitrary commands. Backdoors may also have special capabilities, as follows:

- **Zombies.** A *zombie*, sometimes called a *bot*,[9] is a program that is installed on a system to cause it to attack other systems. The most prevalent type of zombie is a DDoS *agent*; an attacker can issue remote commands to many agents at once so that they perform a coordinated attack against a target. Well-known DDoS agents include Trinoo and Tribe Flood Network.

- **Remote Administration Tools.** As the name implies, a *remote administration tool* (RAT) installed on a system enables a remote attacker to gain access to the system as needed. Most RATs grant full access to the system's functions and data. This may include the ability to watch everything that appears on the system's screen, or to have remote control over the system's devices, such as webcams, microphones, and speakers. Well-known RATs include SubSeven, Back Orifice, and NetBus.

2.7.2 Keystroke Loggers

A *keystroke logger,* also known as a *keylogger*, monitors and records keyboard use.[10] Keystroke loggers can record the information typed into a system, which might include the content of e-mails, usernames and passwords for local or remote systems and applications, and financial information (e.g., credit card number, social security number, personal identification number [PIN]). Some keystroke loggers require the attacker to retrieve the data from the system, whereas other loggers actively transfer the data to another system through e-mail, file transfer, or other means. Examples of keystroke loggers are KeySnatch, Spyster, and KeyLogger Pro.

2.7.3 Rootkits

A *rootkit* is a collection of files that is installed on a system to alter the standard functionality of the system in a malicious and stealthy way. On some operating systems, such as versions of Unix and Linux, rootkits modify or replace dozens or hundreds of files (including system binaries). On other operating systems, such as Windows, rootkits may modify or replace files or may reside in memory only and modify the use of the OS's built-in system calls. Many changes made by a rootkit hide evidence of the rootkit's existence and the changes it has made to the system, making it very difficult to determine that a rootkit is present on a system and identify what the rootkit changed. For example, a rootkit might suppress directory and process listing entries related to its own files. Rootkits are often used to install other types of attacker tools, such as backdoors and keystroke loggers, on a system. Examples of rootkits include LRK5, Knark, Adore, and Hacker Defender.

---

[9]   Although zombies are commonly called bots, the term "bot" is actually a generic term for a program that performs any function automatically. Accordingly, bots can be benign or malicious, and multiple types of malware technically can be referred to as bots. A group of computers running the same type of bot is known as a *botnet*.

[10] Some keystroke loggers offer additional data recording capabilities, such as performing screen captures.

GUIDE TO MALWARE INCIDENT PREVENTION AND HANDLING

2.7.4 Web Browser Plug-Ins

A *Web browser plug-in* provides a way for certain types of content to be displayed or executed through a Web browser. Attackers sometimes create malicious plug-ins that act as spyware. When installed in a browser, these plug-ins can monitor all use of the browser, such as which Web sites and pages a user visits, and report the use to an external party. Because plug-ins are loaded automatically when a Web browser is started, they provide an easy way to monitor Web activity on a system. Some malicious Web browser plug-ins are spyware dialers, which use modem lines to dial phone numbers without the user's permission or knowledge. Many of the dialers are configured to call numbers that have high per-minute charges, while others make nuisance calls to numbers such as emergency services (i.e., "911").[11]

2.7.5 E-Mail Generators

Malware can deliver an *e-mail generating program* to a system, which can be used to create and send large quantities of e-mail to other systems without the user's permission or knowledge. Attackers often configure e-mail generators to send malware, spyware, spam, or other unwanted content to e-mail addresses on a predetermined list.

2.7.6 Attacker Toolkits

Many attackers use toolkits containing several different types of utilities and scripts that can be used to probe and attack systems. Once a system has been compromised through malware or other means, an attacker might download and install a toolkit on the system. The toolkit can then be used to further compromise the system on which it has been installed, or to attack other systems. Types of programs typically found in an attacker toolkit are as follows:

- **Packet Sniffers.** *Packet sniffers* are designed to monitor network traffic on wired or wireless networks and capture packets. Packet sniffers generally can be configured the sniffer to capture all packets or only those with particular characteristics (e.g., certain TCP ports, certain source or destination IP addresses). Most packet sniffers are also *protocol analyzers*, which means that they can reassemble streams from individual packets and decode communications that use any of hundreds or thousands of different protocols.

- **Port Scanners.** A *port scanner* is a program that attempts to determine remotely which ports on systems are open (i.e., whether systems allow connections through those ports). Port scanners help attackers to identify potential targets.

- **Vulnerability Scanners.** A *vulnerability scanner* is a program that looks for vulnerabilities on either the local system or on remote systems. Vulnerability scanners help attackers to find hosts that they can exploit successfully.

- **Password Crackers.** Various utilities are available that can crack OS and application passwords. Most cracking utilities can attempt to guess passwords, as well as performing brute force attempts that try every possible password. The time needed for a brute force attack on an encoded or encrypted password can vary greatly, depending on the type of encryption used and the sophistication of the password itself

- **Remote Login Programs.** Attacker toolkits often contain programs such as SSH and telnet that can be used to log in to other systems remotely. Attackers can use these programs for many purposes, such as controlling compromised systems and transferring data between systems.

---

[11] Some dialers are in forms other than Web browser plug-ins, such as Trojan horses.

■ **Attacks.** Attacker toolkits often contain a variety of utilities and scripts that can launch attacks against the local system or remote systems. The attacks may have a variety of purposes, including compromising a system or causing a denial of service.

Many of the programs found in attacker toolkits can be used for both benign and malicious purposes. For example, packet sniffers and protocol analyzers are often used by network administrators to troubleshoot network communication problems, but they can also be used by attackers to eavesdrop on others' communications. Security administrators might use password crackers to test the strength of users' passwords on a system. Some of the types of programs often found in attacker toolkits are built in to certain operating systems as diagnostic or administrative utilities. Therefore, the presence of any of these types of programs on a system does not necessarily indicate that anything malicious has occurred.

2.8 Non-Malware Threats

This section briefly discusses two forms of non-malware threats that are often associated with malware. First, it explains the technique of phishing, which is used to trick users into revealing financial information and other sensitive data. Phishing attacks frequently place malware or other attacker tools onto systems. The second topic is virus hoaxes, which are false warnings of new malware threats. Both phishing and virus hoaxes rely entirely on *social engineering*, which is a general term for attackers trying to trick people into revealing sensitive information or performing certain actions, such as downloading and executing files that appear to be benign but are actually malicious. Although phishing and virus hoaxes are generally not considered forms of malware, they are often discussed in conjunction with malware, so for completeness this section covers them briefly.

2.8.1 Phishing

Phishing refers to use of deceptive computer-based means to trick individuals into disclosing sensitive personal information.[12] To perform a phishing attack, an attacker creates a Web site or e-mail that looks as if it is from a well-known organization, such as an online business, credit card company, or financial institution.[13] The fraudulent e-mails and Web sites are intended to deceive users into disclosing personal data, usually financial information. For example, phishers might seek usernames and passwords for online banking sites, as well as bank account numbers.

Phishing attacks aid criminals in a wide range of illegal activities, including identity theft and fraud. They can also be used to install malware and attacker tools on a user's system. Common methods of installing malware in phishing attacks include phony banner advertising and popup windows on Web sites. Users who click on the fake ads or popup windows may unknowingly permit keystroke loggers to be installed on their systems. These tools can allow a phisher to record a user's personal data and passwords for any and all Web sites that the user visits, rather than just for a single Web site.

2.8.2 Virus Hoaxes

As the name implies, virus hoaxes are false virus warnings. The phony viruses are usually described as being of devastating magnitude and requiring immediate action to adequately protect computer resources from infection. The majority of virus alerts that are sent via e-mail among users are actually hoaxes. Virus hoaxes are often forwarded among users for months or even years because the users believe they

---

[12] For more information on phishing, including examples of recent phishing attacks, visit the Anti-Phishing Working Group Web site, located at http://www.antiphishing.org/. Another good resource is *How Not to Get Hooked by a "Phishing" Scam*, from the Federal Trade Commission (FTC), available at http://www.ftc.gov/bcp/conline/pubs/alerts/phishingalrt.htm.
[13] Phishing attacks are not limited to traditional computers; they may also target mobile computing devices such as cell phones and personal digital assistants (PDA).

are helping others by distributing these warnings. Although the hoaxes usually do not cause damage, some virus hoaxes are malicious and direct users to alter OS settings or delete files, which could cause security or operational problems. Virus hoaxes can also be time consuming for organizations, because many hoax recipients contact technical support staff to warn them of the new threat or to ask for guidance. One well-known virus hoax is Good Times.

2.9 History of Malware

To understand the relative importance of different types of malware, it is useful to know the relevant history of malware.[14]

The concept of the computer virus was actually formed in the early days of computing. The earliest viruses were benign pranks; malicious viruses did not surface publicly until the early 1980s. The first worms, created in the late 1970s, were also benign, intended to perform system maintenance. Malware did not become common until the late 1980s. In that period, its most common form was compiled viruses, particularly boot sector viruses. At that time, virus writers also created several obfuscation techniques so that their viruses could avoid detection. In 1988, the infamous Morris worm was released, disrupting thousands of networked computers. Trojan horses began to surface in the mid-1980s.

During the early 1990s, the malware situation remained largely unchanged, with compiled viruses continuing to be the prevalent form of malicious code. However, during the latter half of the 1990s, several important changes in computing created new opportunities for malware. First, the number of personal computers greatly increased. In addition, the use of e-mail clients and software with macro languages, such as word processors and spreadsheets, became widespread. Accordingly, virus writers began developing interpreted viruses and spreading them through e-mail, as well as developing self-contained worms with similar capabilities. Interpreted viruses had the advantage of being generally easier to write and modify than compiled viruses, allowing less skilled programmers to create viruses. Two interpreted malware attacks, the Melissa virus (in 1999) and the LoveLetter worm (in 2000), each affected millions of systems. Trojan horse and RAT combinations, such as BackOrifice, also became popular in the late 1990s.

Since 2000, worms have been the prevalent form of malware. Virus writers often favor worms over viruses because worms can spread much more quickly. Among viruses, boot sector viruses have become relatively uncommon, primarily because of the declining usage of floppy disks[15]; in contrast, macro viruses have become the most common virus type. In 2001, the first major blended attack, Nimda, was released, causing major disruptions. Nimda had characteristics of viruses, worms, and malicious mobile code. More recently, malicious mobile code attacks have become increasingly common, largely because of the prevalence of Web browsers and HTML-based e-mail; however, malicious mobile code is still not as common as worms. Another trend is that more instances of malware, including worms, Trojan horses, and malicious mobile code, deliver attacker tools, such as rootkits, keystroke loggers, and backdoors, to infected systems.

---

[14] The sources of information for this section are *Threat Assessment of Malicious Code and Human Threats* by Lawrence E. Bassham and W. Timothy Polk of NIST (http://csrc.nist.gov/publications/nistir/threats/subsubsection3_3_1_1.html); *A Short History of Computer Viruses and Attacks* by Brian Krebs of the Washington Post (http://www.washingtonpost.com/ac2/wp-dyn/A50636-2002Jun26?start=15&per=18); and *Computer Virus Timeline* by Infoplease (http://www.infoplease.com/ipa/A0872842.html).

[15] Boot sector viruses were most prevalent in the early 1990s, when floppy disks were the most common medium for storing files and transferring files between systems. As faster methods of transferring files became more popular, such as e-mail and file sharing software, attackers started developing other types of malware that took advantage of these faster methods to spread much more rapidly. However, boot sector viruses still do occur, and CDs, DVDs, and other removable media present in systems during boot can infect systems with such viruses.

2.10 Summary

Malware has become the greatest external threat to most systems, causing damage and requiring extensive recovery efforts within most organizations. Malware is divided into the following major categories:

- **Viruses.** A virus self-replicates by inserting copies of itself into host programs or data files. Viruses are often triggered through user interaction, such as opening a file or running a program. Viruses can be divided into the following two subcategories:

  - **Compiled Viruses.** A compiled virus is executed by an operating system. Types of compiled viruses include file infector viruses, which attach themselves to executable programs; boot sector viruses, which infect the master boot records of hard drives or the boot sectors of removable media; and multipartite viruses, which combine the characteristics of file infector and boot sector viruses.

  - **Interpreted Viruses.** Interpreted viruses are executed by an application. Within this subcategory, macro viruses take advantage of the capabilities of applications' macro programming language to infect application documents and document templates, while scripting viruses infect scripts that are understood by scripting languages processed by services on the OS.

- **Worms.** A worm is a self-replicating, self-contained program that usually executes itself without user intervention. Worms are divided into two categories:

  - **Network Service Worms.** A network service worm takes advantage of a vulnerability in a network service to propagate itself and infect other systems.

  - **Mass Mailing Worms.** A mass mailing worm is similar to an e-mail–borne virus but is self-contained, rather than infecting an existing file.

- **Trojan Horses.** A Trojan horse is a self-contained, nonreplicating program that, while appearing to be benign, actually has a hidden malicious purpose. Trojan horses either replace existing files with malicious versions or add new malicious files to systems. They often deliver other attacker tools to systems.

- **Malicious Mobile Code.** Malicious mobile code is software with malicious intent that is transmitted from a remote system to a local system and then executed on the local system, typically without the user's explicit instruction. Popular languages for malicious mobile code include Java, ActiveX, JavaScript, and VBScript.

- **Blended Attacks.** A blended attack uses multiple infection or transmission methods. For example, a blended attack could combine the propagation methods of viruses and worms.

- **Tracking Cookies.** A tracking cookie is a persistent cookie that is accessed by many Web sites, allowing a third party to create a profile of a user's behavior. Tracking cookies are often used in conjunction with Web bugs, which are tiny graphics on Web sites that are referenced within the HTML content of a Web page or e-mail. The only purpose of the graphic is to collect information about the user viewing the content.

- **Attacker Tools.** Various types of attacker tools might be delivered to a system as part of a malware infection or other system compromise. These tools allow attackers to have unauthorized access to or use of infected systems and their data, or to launch additional attacks. Popular types of attacker tools are as follows:

– **Backdoors.** A backdoor is a malicious program that listens for commands on a certain TCP or UDP port. Most backdoors allow an attacker to perform a certain set of actions on a system, such as acquiring passwords or executing arbitrary commands. Types of backdoors include zombies (also known as bots), which are installed on a system to cause it to attack other systems, and remote administration tools, which are installed on a system to enable a remote attacker to gain access to the system's functions and data as needed.

– **Keystroke Loggers.** A keystroke logger monitors and records keyboard use. Some require the attacker to retrieve the data from the system, whereas other loggers actively transfer the data to another system through e-mail, file transfer, or other means.

– **Rootkits.** A rootkit is a collection of files that is installed on a system to alter its standard functionality in a malicious and stealthy way. A rootkit typically makes many changes to a system to hide the rootkit's existence, making it very difficult to determine that the rootkit is present and to identify what the rootkit has changed.

– **Web Browser Plug-Ins.** A Web browser plug-in provides a way for certain types of content to be displayed or executed through a Web browser. Attackers often create malicious Web browser plug-ins that act as spyware and monitor all use of the browser.

– **E-Mail Generators.** An e-mail generating program can be used to create and send large quantities of e-mail, such as malware, spyware, and spam, to other systems without the user's permission or knowledge.

– **Attacker Toolkits.** Many attackers use toolkits containing several different types of utilities and scripts that can be used to probe and attack systems, such as packet sniffers, port scanners, vulnerability scanners, password crackers, remote login programs, and attack programs and scripts.

In addition to malware, there are also a few common non-malware threats that are often associated with malware. Phishing uses computer-based means to trick users into revealing financial information and other sensitive data. Phishing attacks frequently place malware or attacker tools on systems. An additional malicious content threat is virus hoaxes—false warnings of new malware threats.

Table 2-1 compares viruses, worms, Trojan horses, malicious mobile code, tracking cookies, and attacker tools on the basis of key characteristics. Because blended attacks may combine features of any combination of the other malware categories, their specific characteristics cannot be defined using these categories.

Table 2-1. Differentiating Malware Categories

Characteristic	Virus	Worm	Trojan Horse	Malicious Mobile Code	Tracking Cookie	Attacker Tools
Is it self-contained?	No	Yes	Yes	No	Yes	Yes
Is it self-replicating?	Yes	Yes	No	No	No	No
What is its propagation method?	User interaction	Self-propagation	N/A	N/A	N/A	N/A

3.   Malware Incident Prevention

This section presents recommendations for preventing malware incidents within an organization. The four main elements of prevention are policy, awareness, vulnerability mitigation, and threat mitigation. Ensuring that policies address malware prevention provides a basis for implementing preventive controls. Establishing and maintaining general malware awareness programs for all users, as well as specific awareness training for the IT staff directly involved in malware prevention–related activities, are critical to reducing the number of incidents that occur through human error. Expending effort on vulnerability mitigation can eliminate some possible attack vectors. Implementing a combination of threat mitigation techniques and tools, such as antivirus software and firewalls, can prevent threats from successfully attacking systems and networks. Sections 3.1 through 3.4 address each of these areas in detail and explain that organizations should implement guidance from each category of recommendations to create an effective layered defense against malware.

When planning an approach to malware prevention, organizations should be mindful of the attack vectors that are most likely to be used currently and in the near future. They should also consider how well-controlled their systems are (e.g., managed environment, non-managed environment); this has significant bearing on the effectiveness of various preventive approaches. In addition, organizations should incorporate existing capabilities, such as antivirus software deployments and patch management programs, into their malware prevention efforts. However, organizations should be aware that no matter how much effort they put into malware incident prevention, incidents will still occur (e.g., previously unknown types of threats, human error). For this reason, as described in Section 4, organizations should have robust malware incident handling capabilities to limit the damage that malware can cause and restore data and services efficiently.

3.1   Policy

Organizations should ensure that their policies address prevention of malware incidents. These policy statements should be used as the basis for additional malware prevention efforts, such as user and IT staff awareness, vulnerability mitigation, and threat mitigation (described in Sections 3.2 through 3.4, respectively). If an organization does not state malware prevention considerations clearly in its policies, it is unlikely to perform malware prevention activities consistently and effectively throughout the organization. Malware prevention–related policy should be as general as possible to provide flexibility in policy implementation and reduce the need for frequent policy updates, but also specific enough to make the intent and scope of the policy clear. Although some organizations have separate malware policies, many malware prevention considerations belong in other policies, such as acceptable use policies, so a separate malware policy might duplicate some of the content of other policies.[16] Malware prevention–related policy should include provisions related to remote workers—both those using systems controlled by the organization and those using systems outside of the organization's control (e.g., contractor computers, employees' home computers, business partners' computers, mobile devices).

Common malware prevention–related policy considerations include the following:[17]

- Requiring the scanning of media from outside of the organization for malware before they can be used

---

[16] For example, many acceptable use policies state that the organization's computing resources should be used only in support of the organization. Personal use of computing resources is a common source of malware incidents; however, because there are several other reasons why an organization might not want to permit personal use of computing resources, this policy consideration is more appropriately addressed in the organization's acceptable use policy than a malware policy.
[17] Although all of these considerations are intended to help organizations prevent malware incidents, many of them could also be helpful in detecting or containing incidents.

■ Requiring that e-mail file attachments, including compressed files (e.g., .zip files), be saved to local drives or media and scanned before they are opened

■ Forbidding the sending or receipt of certain types of files (e.g., .exe files) via e-mail and allowing certain additional file types to be blocked for a period of time in response to an impending malware threat

■ Restricting or forbidding the use of unnecessary software, such as user applications that are often used to transfer malware (e.g., personal use of external instant messaging, desktop search engine, and peer-to-peer file sharing services), and services that are not needed or duplicate the organization-provided equivalents (e.g., e-mail) and might contain additional vulnerabilities that could be exploited by malware

■ Restricting the use of administrator-level privileges by users, which helps to limit the privileges available to malware introduced to systems by users

■ Requiring that systems be kept up-to-date with OS and application upgrades and patches

■ Restricting the use of removable media (e.g., floppy disks, compact discs [CD], Universal Serial Bus [USB] flash drives), particularly on systems that are at high risk of infection, such as publicly accessible kiosks

■ Specifying which types of preventive software (e.g., antivirus software, spyware detection, and removal utilities) are required for each type of system (e.g., file server, e-mail server, proxy server, workstation, personal digital assistant [PDA]) and application (e.g., e-mail client, Web browser), and listing the high-level requirements for configuring and maintaining the software (e.g., software update frequency, system scan scope and frequency)

■ Permitting access to other networks (including the Internet) only through organization-approved and secured mechanisms

■ Requiring firewall configuration changes to be approved through a formal process

■ Specifying which types of mobile code may be used from various sources (e.g., internal Web servers, other organizations' Web servers)

■ Restricting the use of mobile devices on trusted networks.

3.2 Awareness

An effective awareness program explains proper rules of behavior for use of an organization's IT systems and information. Accordingly, awareness programs should include guidance to users about malware incident prevention, which can help reduce the frequency and severity of malware incidents. All users within an organization should be made aware of the ways in which malware enters systems, infects them, and spreads; the risks that malware poses; the inability of technical controls to prevent all incidents; and the importance of users in preventing incidents. Awareness activities should also take into account the characteristics of different environments, such as those encountered by telecommuters and traveling employees in hotels, coffee shops, and other external locations. In addition, the organization's awareness program should cover the malware incident prevention considerations in the organization's policies and procedures, as described in Section 3.1, as well as generally recommended practices for avoiding malware incidents. Examples of such practices are as follows:

■ Not opening suspicious e-mails or e-mail attachments from unknown or known senders

- Not clicking on suspicious Web browser popup windows

- Not visiting Web sites that are at least somewhat likely to contain malicious content

- Not opening files with file extensions that are likely to be associated with malware (e.g., *.bat, .com, .exe, .pif, .vbs*)

- Not disabling the additional security control mechanisms (e.g., antivirus software, spyware detection and removal utility, personal firewall)

- Not using administrator-level accounts for regular system operation

- Not downloading or executing applications from untrusted sources.

As described in Section 4, organizations should also make users aware of policies and procedures that apply to malware incident handling, such as how to identify if a system may be infected, how to report a suspected infection, and what users might need to do to assist with incident handling (e.g., updating antivirus software, scanning systems for malware). Users should be made aware of how notices of major malware incidents will be communicated and given a way to verify the authenticity of all such notices. In addition, users should be aware of changes that might be temporarily made to the environment to contain an incident, such as disconnecting infected systems from networks and blocking certain types of e-mail attachments.

As part of awareness activities, organizations should educate their users on the techniques that criminals use to trick users into disclosing information. Organizations should also provide users with recommendations for avoiding phishing attacks, which are described in Section 2.8.1. Examples of such recommendations are as follows:

- Never reply to e-mail requests for financial or personal information. Organizations should not ask for such information by e-mail, because e-mail is susceptible to monitoring by unauthorized parties. Instead, call the organization at its legitimate phone number, or type the organization's known Web site address into a Web browser. Do not use the contact information provided in the e-mail.

- Do not provide passwords, PINs, or other access codes in response to e-mails or unsolicited popup windows. Only enter such information into the organization's legitimate Web site.

- Do not open suspicious e-mail file attachments, even if they come from known senders. If an unexpected attachment is received, contact the sender (preferably by a method other than e-mail, such as phone) to confirm that the attachment is legitimate.

- Do not respond to any suspicious or unwanted e-mails. (Asking to have an e-mail address removed from a malicious party's mailing list confirms the existence and active use of that e-mail address, potentially leading to additional attack attempts.)

Although user awareness programs help to reduce the frequency and severity of malware incidents, their impact is typically minor compared to that of the technical controls for vulnerability and threat mitigation described in Sections 3.3 and 3.4. An organization should not rely on user awareness as its primary method of preventing malware incidents; instead, the awareness program should supplement the technical controls to provide additional protection against incidents.

The awareness program for users should also serve as the foundation for awareness activities for the IT staff involved in malware incident prevention, such as security, system, and network administrators. All

IT staff members should have some basic level of awareness regarding malware prevention, and individuals should be trained in the malware prevention–related tasks that pertain to their areas of responsibility. In addition, on an ongoing basis, some IT staff members (most likely, some members of the security or incident response teams) should receive and review bulletins on new malware threats, assess the likely risk to the organization, and inform the necessary IT staff members of the new threat so that infections can be prevented. IT staff awareness activities related to malware incident handling are discussed in Section 4.

3.3 Vulnerability Mitigation

As described in Section 2, malware often attacks systems by exploiting vulnerabilities in operating systems, services, and applications. Consequently, mitigating vulnerabilities is very important to the prevention of malware incidents, particularly when malware is released shortly after the announcement of a new vulnerability, or even before a vulnerability is publicly acknowledged. A vulnerability can usually be mitigated by one or more methods, such as applying patches to update the software, or reconfiguring the software (e.g., disabling a vulnerable service).

Because of the challenges that vulnerability mitigation presents, including handling the continual discovery of new vulnerabilities, organizations should have documented policy, processes, and procedures for vulnerability mitigation and should also consider creating a vulnerability management program to assist in mitigation efforts.[18] They also should evaluate their vulnerabilities constantly so that vulnerability mitigation efforts are prioritized properly. Information on new vulnerabilities and major new malware threats should be collected through a combination of sources, such as advisories from incident response teams and organizations (e.g., the U.S. Computer Emergency Readiness Team [US-CERT]), vendor security bulletins, and malware advisories from antivirus software vendors.[19] Organizations also should establish a mechanism for evaluating the new vulnerability and threat information, determining appropriate mitigation methods, and distributing the information to the appropriate parties. Organizations should also have a method for tracking the progress of mitigation efforts.

Organizations should approach mitigation of vulnerabilities using the principle of layered defense, since no single measure will be sufficient to mitigate most vulnerabilities. Sections 3.3.1 through 3.3.3 describe three general categories of vulnerability mitigation techniques—patch management, least privilege, and other host hardening measures.[20] In addition to vulnerability mitigation, organizations should also perform threat mitigation actions that focus on stopping malware from having the opportunity to attempt to exploit vulnerabilities. Security tools such as antivirus software can detect and stop malware before it reaches its intended targets. Threat mitigation is particularly important for instances of malware that do not exploit vulnerabilities, such as attacks that rely on tricking users into running malicious files. Threat mitigation is also critical for situations where a major new threat is likely to attack an organization soon and the organization does not have an acceptable vulnerability mitigation option. For example, there might not be a patch available for a new vulnerability. Section 3.4 focuses on security tools that are useful for threat mitigation.

---

[18] More information on vulnerability mitigation, including patch management, is available from NIST SP 800-40, *Creating a Patch and Vulnerability Management Program*, available from http://csrc.nist.gov/publications/nistpubs/index.html.

[19] In October 2005, the MITRE Corporation announced its Common Malware Enumeration (CME) project, which establishes a standard identifier for each major new malware threat. Antivirus vendors often use different names to refer to the same malware, which can be confusing to people reading vendor bulletins or receiving alerts from multiple antivirus products. The intent of the CME project is to provide standard identifiers that can be used by all antivirus products. More information on CME is available at http://cme.mitre.org/.

[20] There are many other steps that can also be helpful in mitigating vulnerabilities. The techniques listed here could apply to securing nearly any system, but are particularly helpful for protecting against malware.

3.3.1 Patch Management

Applying patches to systems is the most common way of mitigating known vulnerabilities in operating systems and applications. Patch management involves several steps, including assessing the criticality of the patches and the impact of applying or not applying them, testing the patches thoroughly, applying the patches in a controlled manner, and documenting the patch assessment and decision process. It is becoming increasingly challenging to deploy patches quickly enough to prevent incidents—the time from the announcement of a major new vulnerability that is a good candidate for malware-based exploitation to the release of malware targeting that vulnerability has decreased from months to weeks or days. Because it often takes weeks to test new patches properly, it is also often not possible or prudent to deploy patches organization-wide immediately. In some cases, it is safer to use other vulnerability mitigation techniques or threat mitigation instead of patching. In addition, even when a patch has been tested thoroughly and found to be acceptable, it is often challenging to ensure that it is applied to every vulnerable machine in the organization, particularly remote systems (e.g., telecommuters). Nevertheless, applying patches is one of the most effective ways of reducing the risk of malware incidents, and many instances of malware have succeeded because systems were not patched in a timely manner. Patch management is also key to incident handling, as described in Section 4.

3.3.2 Least Privilege

The principle of least privilege refers to configuring hosts to provide only the minimum rights to the appropriate users, processes, and hosts. Least privilege can be helpful in preventing malware incidents, because malware often requires administrator-level privileges to exploit vulnerabilities successfully. If an incident does occur, prior application of least privilege might minimize the amount of damage that the malware can cause. Least privilege is usually employed on an organization's servers and network devices, and is sometimes employed on users' desktops and laptops (most often to remove administrator-level privileges from users). Least privilege can be resource-intensive to implement and support; for example, users might not be able to install OS or application updates without administrative privileges. Least privilege is more likely to be applied within managed environments than non-managed ones.

3.3.3 Other Host Hardening Measures

In addition to keeping hosts properly patched and following the principle of least privilege where appropriate, organizations should also consider implementing other host hardening measures that can further reduce the possibility of malware incidents. Examples of such measures are as follows:

- Disabling or removing unneeded services (particularly network services), which could contain vulnerabilities

- Eliminating unsecured file shares, which are a common infection mechanism for worms

- Removing or changing default usernames and passwords for OSs and applications, which could be used by malware to gain unauthorized access to systems

- Requiring authentication before allowing access to a network service

- Disabling automatic execution of binaries and scripts.

Organizations should consider using OS and application configuration guides or checklists to help administrators secure hosts consistently and effectively.[21] Configuration guides and checklists typically contain recommendations for settings that improve the default level of security and may also contain step-by-step instructions for securing systems. Organizations should also perform periodic vulnerability assessments to identify unmitigated vulnerabilities on systems and develop plans for addressing the vulnerabilities.[22] Even if all known vulnerabilities on a system have been addressed, periodic vulnerability assessments are still important because normal system maintenance activities could inadvertently cause a vulnerability mitigation measure to be removed. For example, installing a patch could accidentally remove another patch or change a security setting to an insecure default.

3.4 Threat Mitigation

As noted in Section 3.3, in addition to their vulnerability mitigation efforts, organizations should perform threat mitigation to detect and stop malware before it can affect its targets. This section describes several types of security tools that can mitigate malware threats: antivirus software, spyware detection and removal utilities, intrusion prevention systems (IPS), and firewalls and routers. For each of these categories, the section also describes typical features, the types of malware and attack vectors the tools address, and the methods they use to detect and stop malware. Recommendations and guidance for implementing, configuring, and maintaining the tools are also provided, as well as explanations of the tools' shortcomings and the ways in which they complement other tools. In addition, the section discusses client and server application settings that can be helpful in mitigating threats.

3.4.1 Antivirus Software

Antivirus software is the most commonly used technical control for malware threat mitigation. For operating systems and applications that are frequently targeted by malware, antivirus software has become a necessity for preventing incidents. There are many brands of antivirus software, with most providing similar protection through the following recommended capabilities:

- Scanning critical system components such as startup files and boot records.

- Watching real-time activities on systems to check for suspicious activity; a common example is scanning all e-mail attachments for known viruses as e-mails are sent and received. Antivirus software should be configured to perform real-time scans of each file as it is downloaded, opened, or executed, which is known as *on-access scanning*.

- Monitoring the behavior of common applications, such as e-mail clients, Web browsers, file transfer programs, and instant messaging software. Antivirus software should monitor activity involving the applications most likely to be used to infect systems or spread malware to other systems.

- Scanning files for known viruses. Antivirus software on systems should be configured to scan all hard drives regularly to identify any file system infections and, optionally, to scan other storage media as well. Users should also be able to launch a scan manually as needed, which is known as *on-demand scanning*.

---

[21] Checklists and implementation guides for various operating systems and applications are available from NIST at http://csrc.nist.gov/pcig/cig.html. Also, see NIST SP 800-70, *Security Configuration Checklists Program for IT Products*, available at http://csrc.nist.gov/checklists/.

[22] For more information on vulnerability assessments, see NIST SP 800-42, *Guideline on Network Security Testing*, available from http://csrc.nist.gov/publications/nistpubs/index.html.

- Identifying common types of malware—viruses, worms, Trojan horses, malicious mobile code, and blended threats—as well as attacker tools such as keystroke loggers and backdoors.[23] Most antivirus products are also increasing their support for detecting spyware. As described in Section 3.4.2, spyware detection and removal utilities can be used to supplement antivirus products that do not yet have robust spyware handling capabilities.

- Disinfecting files, which refers to removing malware from within a file, and quarantining files, which means that files containing malware are stored in isolation for future disinfection or examination. Disinfecting a file is generally preferable to quarantining it because the malware is removed and the original file restored; however, many infected files cannot be disinfected. Accordingly, antivirus software should be configured to attempt to disinfect infected files and to either quarantine or delete files that cannot be disinfected.

Sections 3.4.1.1 through 3.4.1.3 provide additional information and recommendations regarding the detection accuracy, placement, and management of antivirus software, as well as the shortcomings of antivirus software.

3.4.1.1 Antivirus Software Detection Accuracy

Antivirus software products detect malware primarily by looking for certain characteristics of known instances of malware. Such sets of characteristics are known as *signatures*. Signatures are highly effective for identifying known malware and are also often a good means of identifying new variants of known malware, such as a macro virus that has been altered slightly from the original. The major antivirus vendors usually release signatures for a significant new threat within several hours—a remarkable feat considering that each vendor must analyze the threat, write a signature, test it, and distribute it, along with documentation.

Because signatures are based on known threats, they are not effective for identifying completely new malware. To address this, antivirus software vendors have incorporated heuristic techniques into their products; these techniques are designed to identify unknown instances of malware by examining many characteristics of files. Commonly used heuristic techniques include searching files for suspicious code sequences and simulating the behavior of a file to look for anomalous activities (i.e., executing a file in a virtual machine and monitoring its actions). Unfortunately, heuristic techniques sometimes misclassify benign content as malicious; this is known as a *false positive*. Because false positives can be very inconvenient for users and support staff, most antivirus products set the use of heuristic techniques to a moderate or low level by default. Although this does reduce the number of false positives, it also increases the frequency that the antivirus software fails to detect a new malware threat; this is known as a *false negative*. No matter what level of heuristic techniques is used, antivirus software cannot achieve highly accurate detection of new malware threats; however, it is excellent at identifying known threats when its signatures are fully up-to-date. Accordingly, antivirus software should be kept current with the latest signature and software updates to improve malware detection.

---

[23] Of all types of malware and attacker tools, rootkits are traditionally the hardest to detect because they often change the OS at the kernel level, which allows them to be concealed from antivirus software. For Windows systems, Microsoft offers a free utility called the Windows Malicious Software Removal Tool that checks for and attempts to remove certain common malware threats, mainly common worms and rootkits. The tool can be installed on systems automatically through Automatic Updates or Microsoft Update, or it can be downloaded or run directly from Microsoft's Web site at http://www.microsoft.com/security/malwareremove/default.mspx. Because the tool is designed to detect only a small number of common threats, it is a supplement to antivirus software, not a replacement. Additional information on the tool is available from Microsoft Knowledge Base (MSKB) article 890830, available at http://support.microsoft.com/?id=890830.

3.4.1.2 Antivirus Software Placement and Management

Because antivirus software is so important for the prevention of malware incidents, NIST strongly recommends that organizations deploy antivirus software on all systems for which satisfactory antivirus software is available.[24] Antivirus software should be installed as soon after OS installation as possible and then updated with the latest signatures and antivirus software patches (to eliminate any known vulnerabilities in the antivirus software itself). The antivirus software should then perform a complete scan of the system to identify any potential infections. To support the security of the system, the antivirus software should be configured and maintained properly so that it continues to be effective at detecting and stopping malware.

In managed environments, organizations should use centrally managed antivirus software that is controlled and monitored regularly by antivirus administrators, who are also typically responsible for acquiring, testing, approving, and delivering antivirus signature and software updates throughout the organization. In general, users should not be able to disable or delete antivirus software from their systems, nor should they be able to alter any critical settings. Antivirus administrators should perform periodic checks to confirm that systems are using current antivirus software and that the software is configured properly. This information is often available through centralized antivirus management software; organizations can also collect it through scans, system checks performed at network login, and other methods. Implementing all of these recommendations should strongly support an organization in having a strong and consistent antivirus deployment across the organization.

In non-managed environments, particularly those in which users have full control over their own systems, antivirus software is likely to be implemented and maintained inconsistently. Organizations with non-managed environments should consider moving to a managed environment. In non-managed environments, organizations should place particular emphasis on awareness activities. The organization should send periodic reminders to local system administrators and users, asking them to update their signatures; perform awareness activities to increase knowledge of the importance of keeping the software up to date; distribute step-by-step instructions for updating systems; and notify local system administrators and users when major new threats emerge that necessitate updating of antivirus signatures. The organization should also encourage system administrators and users to configure their antivirus software so that it automatically checks frequently (at least daily) for antivirus signature and software updates, and downloads and installs updates promptly.

Organizations with centrally managed antivirus deployments should ensure that their implementations have sufficient redundancy and capacity to meet typical and peak needs. For example, organizations could have multiple antivirus servers available for managing antivirus client software and distributing updates to clients. If practical, it might also be beneficial to use multiple unrelated OS platforms for the antivirus servers to reduce the chance that a single attack against the antivirus servers could affect all of

---

[24] The System and Information Integrity (SI) family of security controls in NIST SP 800-53, *Recommended Security Controls for Federal Information Systems*, contains specific recommendations for antivirus software. Control #SI-3, Malicious Code Protection, recommends that an information system "[implement] malicious code protection that includes a capability for automatic updates." It also provides the following supplemental guidance: "The organization employs virus protection mechanisms at critical information system entry and exit points (e.g., firewalls, electronic mail servers, remote-access servers) and at workstations, servers, or mobile computing devices on the network. The organization uses the virus protection mechanisms to detect and eradicate malicious code (e.g., viruses, worms, Trojan horses) transported: (i) by electronic mail, electronic mail attachments, Internet accesses, removable media (e.g., diskettes or compact disks), or other common means; or (ii) by exploiting information system vulnerabilities. The organization updates virus protection mechanisms (including the latest virus definitions) whenever new releases are available in accordance with organizational configuration management policy and procedures. Consideration is given to using virus protection software products from multiple vendors (e.g., using one vendor for boundary devices and servers and another vendor for workstations)." NIST SP 800-53 is available at http://csrc.nist.gov/publications/nistpubs/index.html.

them. Organizations should also consider using a different OS platform for the antivirus servers than for most servers and workstations in the organization. If a single vulnerability affected most servers and workstations in the organization, as well as the antivirus servers, a rapid attack could cause most of the hosts to become infected and make the antivirus servers unavailable for use.

Another possible measure for improving malware prevention is to use multiple antivirus products for key systems, such as e-mail servers. For example, one antivirus vendor might have a new signature available several hours before another vendor, or an organization might have an operational issue with a particular signature update. Another possibility is that an antivirus product itself might contain an exploitable vulnerability; having an alternative product available in such cases could provide protection until the issue with the primary product has been resolved. Because running multiple antivirus products on a single system simultaneously is likely to cause conflicts between the products, if multiple products are used concurrently, they should be installed on separate systems. For example, one antivirus product could be used on perimeter e-mail servers and another on internal e-mail servers. This could provide more effective detection of new threats, but also would necessitate increased administration and training, as well as additional hardware and software costs.

3.4.1.3 Shortcomings of Antivirus Software

Although antivirus software has become a necessity for malware incident prevention, it is not possible for antivirus software to stop all malware incidents. As discussed previously in this section, antivirus software does not excel at stopping previously unknown threats. Once a new threat is recognized, a new signature might be available within hours; however, organizations still need to acquire, test, and deploy the signature. Testing is important because signatures might occasionally cause antivirus software or OS crashes or have other conflicts with systems and applications. Even in a best-case situation, it would take at least a few hours from the recognition of a new threat to the start of deployment of the new signature, leaving a sizable window of opportunity for a new malware threat to infect systems. Signature deployment might also take considerable time; the antivirus servers and networks might not be able to handle updating all of the organization's machines at once. Also, systems that are not connected to the network might not be updated and could become infected (e.g., malware on removable media).

Another challenge for antivirus software is that malware can spread in many ways, including various network protocols and services (e.g., e-mail, file transfers, peer-to-peer file sharing, Web browsing, chat sessions, instant messaging), as well as removable media (e.g., CD, floppy diskette, flash drive). Organizations should use both host-based and network-based antivirus scanning (i.e., from firewalls and e-mail servers) so that threats attempting to enter the organization through the firewall and through hosts behind the firewall (e.g., infected removable media placed into a workstation) are addressed. However, current antivirus software products might not be capable of monitoring every possible transmission mechanism for every system within an organization. For example, antivirus software might not be able to analyze activity involving a new type of application, service, or network protocol. Organizations should also be mindful of use of their networks by systems outside their control, such as employees connecting from home computers through dial-in and virtual private networks (VPN) or business partners connecting from their organizations' systems. These external systems might become infected with malware and attempt to spread that malware using the organization's networks.

3.4.2 Spyware Detection and Removal Utilities

Spyware detection and removal utilities are designed to identify many types of spyware on systems and quarantine or remove spyware files. Unlike antivirus software, which attempts to identify many types of malware, spyware detection and removal utilities specialize in both malware and non-malware forms of spyware. Currently, spyware detection and removal utilities offer more robust spyware handling capabilities than some antivirus programs. Preventing spyware incidents is important, not only because spyware violates users' privacy, but also because it frequently causes functional problems on systems, such as slowing performance or causing application instability.[25] Although some spyware detection and removal utilities specialize in a particular form of malware, such as malicious Web browser plug-ins, most of the utilities offer wider, and similar, ranges of recommended capabilities, as follows:

- Monitoring the behavior of the applications most likely to be used to place spyware onto systems, such as Web browsers and e-mail clients

- Performing regular scans of files, memory, and configuration files for known spyware

- Identifying several types of spyware, including malicious mobile code, Trojan horses, and tracking cookies

- Quarantining or deleting spyware files (because most spyware files are self-contained, disinfection is usually not applicable)

- Monitoring network drivers and Windows shell settings

- Monitoring processes and programs that are loaded automatically at startup

- Preventing several methods of spyware installation, including popup ads, tracking cookies, browser plug-in installations, and browser hijacking.

To mitigate spyware threats, organizations should use either spyware detection and removal utilities or antivirus software with the ability to recognize spyware threats. The software should be used on all systems for which satisfactory software is available.

Spyware detection and removal utilities typically rely on spyware signatures, which are similar to those used by antivirus software. The tools are effective at recognizing known threats and variants of known threats, but have varying capabilities to detect unknown threats. In addition, because spyware detection and removal utilities rely on signatures, the software should be kept current with the latest signature and software updates to improve spyware detection. Spyware detection and removal utilities should be complemented by controls such as antivirus software that can detect other types of malware threats. Organizations should also consider using multiple spyware detection and removal utilities to improve detection of spyware threats.

Spyware detection and removal utilities have only recently begun to offer centralized management and monitoring capabilities. Some utilities do not even offer the ability to check for and download updates automatically, instead relying on users to open the utility and launch the check manually. Organizations considering an enterprise-wide deployment of spyware detection and removal utilities should determine how the utilities can be distributed, configured, and maintained, as well as how their activity can be monitored to identify spyware incidents. Because antivirus software and spyware detection and removal

---

[25] Control #SI-8, Spam and Spyware Protection, from NIST SP 800-53 recommends that an information system "[implement] spam and spyware protection." The supplemental guidance from SI-8 further recommends that "the organization [employ] spam and spyware protection mechanisms at critical information system entry points (e.g., firewalls, electronic mail servers, remote-access servers) and at workstations, servers, or mobile computing devices on the network. The organization uses the spam and spyware protection mechanisms to detect and take appropriate action on unsolicited messages and spyware/adware, respectively, transported by electronic mail, electronic mail attachments, Internet accesses, removable media (e.g., diskettes or compact disks), or other common means. Consideration is given to using spam and spyware protection software products from multiple vendors (e.g., using one vendor for boundary devices and servers and another vendor for workstations)." NIST SP 800-53 is available at http://csrc.nist.gov/publications/nistpubs/index.html.

utilities have many similar characteristics, organizations should generally apply the same considerations to both types of products.

3.4.3 Intrusion Prevention Systems

Network-based intrusion prevention systems (IPS) perform packet sniffing and analyze network traffic to identify and stop suspicious activity.[26] Network-based IPS products are typically deployed *inline*, which means that the software acts like a network firewall. It receives packets, analyzes them, decides whether they should be permitted, and allows acceptable packets to pass through. The network-based IPS architecture allows some attacks to be detected on networks before they reach their intended targets. Most network-based IPS products use a combination of attack signatures and analysis of network and application protocols, which means that they compare network activity for frequently attacked applications (e.g., e-mail servers, Web servers) to expected behavior to identify potentially malicious activity.

Network-based IPS products are used to detect many types of malicious activity besides malware, and typically can detect only a few instances of malware by default, such as recent major worms. However, some IPS products are highly customizable, allowing administrators to create and deploy attack signatures for many major new malware threats in a matter of minutes. Although there are risks in doing this, such as a poorly written signature triggering false positives that block benign activity inadvertently, a custom signature can block a new malware threat hours before antivirus signatures become available. Network-based IPS products can be effective at stopping specific known threats, such as network service worms, and e-mail–borne worms and viruses with easily recognizable characteristics (e.g., subject, attachment filename). However, network-based IPS products are generally not capable of stopping malicious mobile code or Trojan horses. Network-based IPS products might be able to detect and stop some unknown threats through application protocol analysis.

A specialized form of network-based IPS, known as *DDoS attack mitigation software*, attempts to stop attacks by identifying unusual network traffic flows. Although these products are primarily intended to stop DDoS attacks against an organization, they can also be used to identify worm activity and other forms of malware, as well as use of attacker tools such as backdoors and e-mail generators. DDoS attack mitigation software typically works by monitoring normal network traffic patterns, including which hosts communicate with each other using which protocols, and the typical and peak volumes of activity, to establish baselines. The software then monitors network activity to identify significant deviations from the baselines. If malware causes a particularly high volume of network traffic or uses network or application protocols that are not typically seen, DDoS attack mitigation software should be able to detect and block the activity. Another way of limiting some malware incidents is by configuring network devices to limit the maximum amount of bandwidth that can be used by particular hosts or services. Also, some types of network monitoring software can detect and report significant deviations from expected network activity, although this software typically cannot specifically label the activity as malware-related or block it.

Host-based IPS products are similar in principle and purpose to network-based IPSs, except that a host-based IPS product monitors the characteristics of a single host and the events occurring within that host. Examples of activity that might be monitored by host-based IPSs include network traffic, system logs, running processes, file access and modification, and system and application configuration changes. Host-based IPS products often use a combination of attack signatures and knowledge of expected or typical behavior to identify known and unknown attacks on systems. For example, host-based IPS products that

---

[26] Intrusion prevention systems are similar to intrusion detection systems (IDS), except that IPSs can attempt to stop malicious activity, whereas IDSs cannot. This section discusses the use of IPSs, not IDSs, for preventing or containing malware incidents. Section 4 describes how both IPS and IDS technologies can be used for malware incident detection.

monitor attempted changes to files can be effective at detecting viruses attempting to infect files and Trojan horses attempting to replace files, as well as the use of attacker tools, such as rootkits, that often are delivered by malware. If a host-based IPS product monitors the host's network traffic, it offers detection capabilities similar to a network-based IPS's.

Like antivirus software and spyware detection and removal utilities, network-based and host-based IPS products cause false positives and false negatives. IPS software typically offers tuning capabilities, which can improve accuracy; however, the effectiveness of tuning varies widely among products and environments. Because a false positive could cause benign activity to be stopped, organizations should consider the implications of this and consider configuring the IPSs to block activity only for signatures or anomalous condition definitions that are very unlikely to trigger false positives. Most IPS products allow blocking capabilities to be enabled or disabled for each signature or anomalous condition definition. Some organizations disable all blocking capabilities by default and enable them only when facing a major new threat, such as a worm.

For malware prevention, host-based IPS software might be able to improve an organization's ability to detect and stop unknown threats. If an organization can tune host-based IPS software to a high degree of detection accuracy, it can be helpful for stopping unknown threats that cannot be recognized by antivirus software and other technical controls. IPS software can be particularly helpful in identifying threats that use network services that are not monitored by antivirus software, such as Domain Name System (DNS).

For malware threats that generate a high volume of traffic, such as network service worms, network-based IPS products deployed along the network perimeter can significantly reduce the load that the malware places on the organization's networks. Using a combination of antivirus software and IPS software not only can improve the overall malware incident prevention rate, but also can be helpful in splitting the load of malware handling between two sets of technical controls. During a major incident, antivirus software alone can become overloaded due to the number of malware events; sharing the work among multiple types of controls can reduce slowdowns caused by malware processing.

3.4.4   Firewalls and Routers

Network-based devices such as firewalls and routers, as well as host-based firewall software, examine network traffic and permit or deny it based on a set of rules. A router typically uses a simple set of rules, known as an access control list (ACL), that addresses only the most basic characteristics of network traffic, whereas firewalls offer more robust capabilities. There are two types of firewalls: network firewalls and host-based firewalls. A *network firewall* is a device deployed between networks to restrict which types of traffic can pass from one network to another. A *host-based firewall* is a piece of software running on a single host that can restrict incoming and outgoing network activity for that host only. Both types of firewalls can be useful for preventing malware incidents. Sections 3.4.4.1 and 3.4.4.2 discuss network and host-based firewalls, respectively, while Section 3.4.4.3 briefly discusses routers.

3.4.4.1   Network Firewalls

Organizations typically use one or more network firewalls at their network perimeter to provide protection from external threats. Network firewalls work by comparing network traffic to a set of rules, each of which typically specifies a network or application protocol and the source and destination of the communication. For example, a rule might permit e-mail to reach the organization's e-mail server from external hosts. Accordingly, network firewalls can be effective at stopping network service worms that target a particular service or service port number, especially if the service or port is not widely used by the organization. Because network firewalls can restrict both incoming and outgoing traffic, they can also be used to stop certain worm infections within the organization from spreading to external systems.

To prevent malware incidents, organizations should implement *deny by default* rulesets, meaning that the firewalls deny all incoming and outgoing traffic that is not expressly permitted. With such rulesets in place, malware could not spread using services deemed unnecessary to the organization.[27] To reduce the spread of worms, it is particularly important to consider placing strict limits on the types of traffic that external systems (e.g., telecommuters' home systems, business partners' systems) can send on the organization's networks. Organizations should also ensure that their network firewalls perform egress and ingress filtering. *Ingress filtering* is the process of blocking incoming packets that should not enter a network, such as those from false IP addresses (e.g., packets with reserved or unassigned source addresses). *Egress filtering* blocks outgoing packets that should not exit a network, such as those from false IP addresses (e.g., packets with internal network source addresses accidentally leaving the organization and entering the Internet).[28] Worms often generate random IP addresses as they attempt to spread; therefore, blocking packets with false IP addresses should reduce the number of worms that enter an organization's internal networks. Organizations should review their network firewall rulesets regularly to validate each rule and identify any activity permitted by the ruleset that no longer should be permitted.

Firewall software itself does not look for attacks contained within network communications; however, firewalls often run additional software that can do so. For example, many firewalls also run intrusion prevention or antivirus software to look for attacks in certain types of communications, such as e-mail and Web traffic. Some firewalls also act as proxies; a *proxy* receives a request from a client, then sends a request on the client's behalf to the desired destination. When a proxy is used, each successful connection attempt actually results in the creation of two separate connections: one between the client and the firewall, and another between the firewall and the true destination. Some proxies perform basic analysis and validation of application protocols, such as Hypertext Transfer Protocol (HTTP), and can reject client requests that appear to be invalid, which might include some instances of malware. Such proxies are also known as application layer firewalls.

Network firewalls are also commonly used to perform *network address translation* (NAT), which is the process of mapping addresses on one network to addresses on another network. NAT is most often performed by mapping private addresses from an internal network to one or more public addresses on a network that is connected to the Internet. When private addresses are used for hosts and mapped to public addresses through NAT, external hosts cannot initiate connections directly to the internal hosts because private addresses are not routable across the Internet. This can be helpful in preventing network service worms on Internet-based hosts from contacting hosts within the organization.

When a major new malware threat targeting a network service is impending, organizations might need to rely on network firewalls to prevent an incident, particularly if antivirus software and intrusion prevention software do not monitor the targeted service. To prepare for worst-case situations, organizations should be ready to add or change firewall rules quickly to prevent a network service–based malware incident. Firewall rules might also be helpful in stopping malware that relies on particular IP addresses, such as a worm that downloads Trojan horses from one of ten external hosts. Adding a rule that blocks all activity involving the external hosts' IP addresses could prevent the Trojan horses from reaching the organization.

---

[27]   The use of some services cannot be blocked easily through firewall rulesets. For example, some peer-to-peer file sharing services and instant messaging services can use port numbers designated for other services, such as HTTP or Simple Mail Transfer Protocol (SMTP). Attempting to prevent the use of such services by blocking port numbers might cause legitimate services to be blocked. In such cases, it might be necessary to block access to particular IP addresses that host portions of the services, such as instant messaging servers. Also, as described later in this section, application proxies can identify some instances in which one service is used when another is expected.

[28]   See Internet Engineering Task Force (IETF) Request for Comment (RFC) 2267, *Network Ingress Filtering: Defeating Denial of Service Attacks Which Employ IP Source Address Spoofing*, for more information (http://www.ietf.org/rfc/rfc2267.txt). Information on unassigned IP address ranges is available at http://www.cymru.com/Documents/bogon-list.html.

3.4.4.2 Host-Based Firewalls

Host-based firewalls can restrict incoming and outgoing network activity for individual hosts, which can prevent hosts from becoming infected and stop infected hosts from spreading malware to other hosts. Host-based firewalls for servers typically use rulesets similar to those of network firewalls. Some host-based firewalls for desktops and laptops also use similar rulesets, but most allow or deny activity based on lists of applications. Activity involving any application not on the lists is either denied automatically, or permitted or denied on the basis of the user's response to a prompt asking for a decision about the activity. To prevent malware incidents, organizations should configure host-based firewalls with deny-by-default rulesets for incoming traffic. Organizations should also use deny-by-default rulesets for outgoing traffic, if feasible; however, such rulesets might have a serious negative effect on system usability and user satisfaction.

In addition to restricting network activity based on rules, many host-based firewalls for workstations incorporate antivirus software and intrusion prevention software capabilities, as well as suppressing Web browser popup windows, restricting mobile code, blocking cookies, and identifying potential privacy issues within Web pages and e-mails. Host-based firewalls that integrate these functions can be very effective not only at preventing most types of malware incidents, but also at stopping the spread of malware infections. For example, a host-based firewall with antivirus capabilities can monitor inbound and outbound e-mails for signs of mass mailing viruses or worms and temporarily shut off e-mail services if such activity is detected. Accordingly, host-based firewalls for workstations that offer several types of malware prevention capabilities typically offer the best single host-based technical control for malware threat mitigation, as long as they are configured properly and kept up-to-date at all times with the latest signatures and software updates. Host-based firewalls are particularly important for systems that are network-connected but are not protected by network firewalls and other network-based security controls. Systems that are directly accessible from the Internet should be protected whenever possible through host-based firewalls to prevent network service worms and other threats from connecting to and attacking them.

3.4.4.3 Routers

Whereas firewalls typically restrict incoming and outgoing network activity based on combinations of services and host IP addresses, routers are usually configured with broader, less granular rules. Typically, organizations use one or more routers where the organization's network connects to the Internet; these are known as *Internet border routers*. The routers are usually deployed in front of the organization's main firewalls and perform some basic checks on network activity, such as ingress and egress filtering, that may be helpful in stopping some Internet-based worms from reaching the organization's firewall. Although the firewall should also block such worms, having the Internet border routers do so can take some load off the firewall.

During a major worm incident, organizations might need to reconfigure some of their Internet border routers to block incoming worm activity so that the firewalls do not become overloaded. Routers on internal networks can also be reconfigured to block activity for a particular service from passing between networks; this can prevent infected hosts on one network from spreading malware to other networks. Organizations should be prepared to alter router ACLs quickly when needed to assist in containing worm infections.

3.4.5 Application Settings

Many instances of malware take advantage of features provided by common applications, such as e-mail clients, Web browsers, and word processors. By default, applications often are configured to favor functionality over security. Accordingly, organizations should consider disabling unneeded features and capabilities from applications, particularly those that are commonly exploited by malware, to limit the possible application attack vectors for malware. Organizations should also consider identifying applications that are typical malware propagation methods (e.g., Web browsers, e-mail clients and servers) and configuring them to filter content and stop other activity that is likely to be malicious. Some application settings to consider in malware incident prevention are as follows:

- **Blocking Suspicious E-Mail Attachments.** Many organizations prevent incidents by configuring their e-mail servers (and possibly e-mail clients as well) to identify suspicious e-mail file attachments and either remove the attachments from the e-mails or block the e-mails themselves. For example, many organizations block attachments with file extensions that are often associated with malware (e.g., .pif, .vbs) and suspicious file extension combinations (e.g., .txt.vbs, .htm.exe). Although this can stop unknown threats, it might also inadvertently block legitimate activity. Some organizations alter suspicious e-mail attachment file extensions so that a recipient would have to save the attachment and rename it before running it, which is a good compromise in some environments between functionality and security.

- **Filtering Spam.** Spam is often used for phishing and spyware delivery (e.g., Web bugs often are contained within spam), and it sometimes contains other types of malware. Using spam filtering software on e-mail servers or clients or on network-based appliances can significantly reduce the amount of spam that reaches users, leading to a corresponding decline in spam-triggered malware incidents.

- **Filtering Web Site Content.** Although Web content filtering software is typically thought of as preventing access to materials that are inappropriate for the workplace, it may also contain lists of phishing Web sites and other sites that are known as hostile (i.e., attempting to distribute malware to visitors). Web content filtering software can also block undesired file types, such as by file extension.

- **Limiting Mobile Code Execution.** Applications such as Web browsers and e-mail clients can be configured to permit only the required forms of mobile code (e.g., JavaScript, ActiveX, Java) and to run mobile code only from particular locations (i.e., internal Web sites only). This can be effective at stopping some instances of malicious mobile code, but may also impact the functionality of benign Web sites. Web content filtering software can also be deployed to monitor Web-related network activity and block certain types of mobile code from untrusted locations.

- **Restricting Web Browser Cookies.** Most Web browsers can be configured to prompt users to accept or reject each cookie, or to accept or reject session cookies automatically but prompt users to accept each persistent cookie or reject persistent cookies automatically.[29] Most Web browsers also can be configured to allow cookies to be set only for the Web site the user visited (known as first-party cookies), not for the Web sites of advertisers and other parties (known as third-party cookies). Permitting first-party cookies and blocking third-party cookies can be very helpful in reducing the number of tracking cookies placed onto a system.

- **Blocking Web Browser Popup Windows.** Some popup windows are crafted to look like legitimate system message boxes or Web sites, and can trick users into going to phony Web sites, including sites used for phishing, or authorizing changes to their systems, among other malicious

---

[29] Depending on how the cookie options are configured and which Web sites users visit, prompting users to accept cookies or rejecting certain types of cookies automatically can be very inconvenient for users.

actions. Most Web browsers can block popup windows; others can do so by adding a third-party popup blocker to the Web browser.

- **Preventing Software Installation Within Web Browsers.** Some Web browsers can be configured to prompt the user to approve the installation of software such as Web browser plug-ins. Some browsers can even prevent any Web site from installing software on the client. These settings are particularly helpful for preventing the installation of spyware within Web browsers.

- **Preventing Automatic Loading of E-Mail Images.** Most e-mail clients can be configured not to automatically load graphics contained within e-mails. This is particularly helpful in thwarting e-mail-based Web bugs. With this configuration setting, the outline of an unloaded Web bug appears as a small box within the e-mail, and the user's activity cannot be tracked unless the user chooses to have the image loaded.

- **Altering File Associations.** Many operating systems provide a mechanism for specifying which types of files are associated with certain programs, such as opening .txt files with a text editor. When a user attempts to open a file, the operating system typically checks the default file association and runs the designated application. Although this is convenient for users, it is also helpful to malware; for example, a user could be tricked into attempting to open an e-mail file attachment, which would then be automatically run by the operating system. Many organizations alter the file associations on systems for file types that are most frequently used by malware (e.g., .pif, .vbs) so that the files are not run automatically when users attempt to open them.

- **Restricting Macro Use.** Applications such as word processors and spreadsheets often contain macro languages; macro viruses take advantage of this. Most common applications with macro capabilities offer macro security features that permit macros only from trusted locations or prompt the user to approve or reject each attempt to run a macro.

- **Preventing Open Relaying of E-Mail.** Mass mailing worms sometimes attempt to use an organization's e-mail servers as *open relays*, which means that neither the sender nor the recipients of the e-mail are part of the organization. E-mail servers that permit open relaying can provide mass mailing worms with an easy way to propagate. Organizations should consider configuring their e-mail servers to prevent open relaying and to record all attempts to use them as relays.[30]

Although these application settings can be effective in reducing the frequency of malware incidents, selecting the appropriate settings often is challenging. In most cases, configuring an application to act more securely causes a reduction in functionality. For example, disabling Java support in Web browsers would prevent the organization's Java-based Web applications from running. Accordingly, organizations should carefully consider the implications of each setting and weigh the benefits of improved security against the loss of functionality. Organizations should also be mindful of the variety of client applications in use. For example, client systems might have various versions of multiple Web browsers and multiple e-mail clients installed, each of which has different functionality and possible configuration settings. The organization might also offer a Web-based e-mail client that offers limited functionality and has few security configuration options compared with a standard e-mail client.

In most organizations, implementing and maintaining application settings on servers is relatively easy; doing the same for clients is far more challenging. In highly managed environments, it is usually feasible to control application settings centrally across all clients, but in most other environments it is not practical. Organizations might be able to implement their selected settings on new systems, but could not

---

[30] For more information on open relays and other aspects of e-mail security, see NIST SP 800-45, *Guidelines on Electronic Mail Security*, available at http://csrc.nist.gov/publications/nistpubs/index.html.

ensure that these settings would not be changed or update the settings automatically as needed to respond to changing security and functionality needs. Organizations should consider how application client settings can be implemented, maintained, and checked effectively. In non-managed environments, organizations might need to rely on awareness activities and voluntary participation by users. In managed environments, organizations should consider how needed exceptions to the selected application configuration settings should be approved, implemented, maintained, and periodically validated.

Many of the benefits provided by altering the configuration settings of client applications can also be achieved through the use of host-based firewalls. As described in Section 3.4.4.2, many host-based firewalls can monitor application content through antivirus software, suppress Web browser popup windows, restrict mobile code execution, and block cookies. Many host-based firewalls also can perform spam filtering and Web content filtering. However, host-based firewall features do not address all application settings, so it is most effective to use both a host-based firewall and appropriate application settings for clients.

Being able to alter application configuration settings quickly can be very beneficial in stopping major new threats. For example, suppose that there was a new e-mail-based threat that could not yet be detected by antivirus and intrusion prevention software. In this case, an organization could reconfigure its e-mail server and client settings to delete all e-mails that matched the characteristics of the new threat. Organizations should consider in advance how such settings could be implemented during a malware emergency and establish and maintain appropriate procedures.

3.5 Summary

Organizations should plan and implement an approach to malware incident prevention based on the attack vectors that are most likely to be used, both currently and in the near future. Organizations should choose preventive methods that are well-suited to their environment and systems; for example, a technique that works well in a managed environment might be ineffective in a non-managed environment. An effective approach to malware incident prevention should incorporate policy considerations, awareness programs for users and IT staff, and vulnerability and threat mitigation efforts.

As the basis for additional prevention efforts, organizations should ensure that their policies support the prevention of malware incidents. Common malware prevention–related policy considerations fall into the following three general categories:

- Specifying the acceptable use of systems

- Mitigating vulnerabilities

- Mitigating threats.

Malware prevention–related policy should address considerations related to remote workers using both systems controlled by the organization and systems outside the organization's control.

Organizations should implement awareness programs that include guidance to users on malware incident prevention. All users should be made aware of the ways in which malware spreads, the risks that malware poses, the inability of technical controls to prevent all incidents, and the importance of users in preventing incidents. Awareness programs should also make users aware of policy and procedures that apply to malware incident handling, such as how to report suspected infections and what users might need to do to assist incident handlers. In addition, the organization should conduct awareness activities for IT staff involved in malware incident prevention and provide training in specific tasks.

Organizations should have documented policy, processes, and procedures for vulnerability mitigation to prevent malware from exploiting OS and application vulnerabilities. Because a vulnerability usually can be mitigated by one or more methods, organizations should use a combination of vulnerability mitigation techniques, such as patch management and the principle of least privilege. Patch management is a complex process that can be very effective in mitigating vulnerabilities but might not be feasible for situations in which a new malware threat emerges within days of the announcement of a new vulnerability. Applying the principle of least privilege to systems can stop malware that requires administrator-level privileges for successful exploitation and can reduce the amount of damage that some malware can cause. Organizations should also consider implementing additional host hardening measures, such as eliminating unsecured file shares and disabling or removing unneeded services, to further reduce possible vulnerabilities.

In addition to vulnerability mitigation, organizations should perform threat mitigation efforts to detect and stop malware before it can affect its targets. The following types of technical controls are particularly helpful in threat mitigation:

- Antivirus software is the most commonly used technical control for malware threat mitigation, and has become a necessity for preventing malware incidents. Spyware detection and removal utilities specialize in mitigating both malware and non-malware forms of spyware. Both antivirus software and spyware detection and removal utilities rely on signatures and should be kept updated to improve detection accuracy.

- Network-based IPSs offer limited malware detection capabilities by default, but usually they can be customized to stop specific known threats, such as worms. Host-based IPSs can stop a variety of known and unknown malware-related threats.

- Firewalls can prevent attacks against network services. Host-based firewalls also offer features that monitor application content and functionality to prevent malware incidents from exploiting application vulnerabilities or taking advantage of application features. Routers can be helpful in blocking certain worm threats.

- Organizations can also configure application settings to increase security at the expense of functionality.

4. Malware Incident Response

As defined in NIST SP 800-61, *Computer Security Incident Handling Guide,* the incident response process has four major phases: preparation, detection and analysis, containment/eradication/recovery, and post-incident activity. Figure 4-1 displays this incident response life cycle. This section of the guide builds on the concepts of SP 800-61 by providing additional details about responding to malware incidents.[31]

The initial phase of malware incident response involves performing preparatory activities, such as developing malware-specific incident handling procedures and training programs for incident response teams. As described in Section 3, the preparation phase also involves using policy, awareness activities, vulnerability mitigation, and security tools to reduce the number of malware incidents. Despite these measures, residual risk will inevitably persist, and no solution is foolproof. Detection of malware infections is thus necessary to alert the organization whenever incidents occur. Rapid detection is particularly important for malware incidents because they are more likely than other types of incidents to affect many users and systems within a short time, and faster detection can help reduce the number of infected systems.

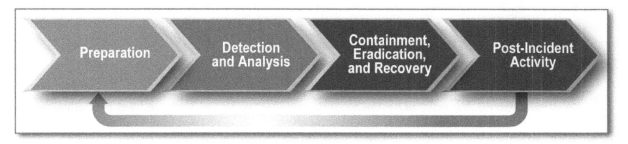

Figure 4-1. Incident Response Life Cycle

For each incident, the organization should act appropriately, based on the severity of the incident, to mitigate its impact by containing it, eradicating infections, and ultimately recovering from the incident. This can be extremely challenging during widespread infections, when a sizable percentage of an organization's systems may be infected at one time. After an incident has been handled, the organization should issue a report that details the cause and cost of the incident and the steps the organization should take to prevent future incidents and to prepare more effectively to handle incidents that do occur.

Although the basic incident handling process is the same for any type of malware incident, widespread infections present many challenges that the standard incident response process does not specifically address. This section of the document focuses on the handling of widespread malware incidents; however, the guidance it provides should also be helpful for those handling less severe malware incidents.

4.1 Preparation

Having a robust incident response capability within an organization is a fundamental part of preparing to handle malware incidents; without such a capability, it can be exceedingly difficult in all but the smallest organizations to contain and eradicate widespread malware infections effectively. Some organizations with particularly high malware handling needs even have a dedicated malware incident response team in

---

[31]   For more information on how to establish an incident response capability, refer to NIST SP 800-61, *Computer Security Incident Handling Guide*, available at http://csrc.nist.gov/publications/nistpubs/index.html.

addition to a general incident response team. Because malware incidents have the potential to cause an extensive negative impact throughout an organization in a matter of minutes, organizations should prepare by developing malware-specific incident handling policies and procedures, which define the roles and responsibilities of all individuals and teams that might be involved in malware incident handling. Regularly conducting malware-oriented training and exercises can be very helpful in ensuring that people are aware of their roles and responsibilities and ensuring that malware policies and procedures are accurate and comprehensive. Exercises for handling widespread infections may be particularly helpful as preparation because such incidents happen relatively infrequently in most organizations, but cause the greatest impact.

Organizations should also perform other preparatory measures to ensure that they are capable of responding effectively to malware incidents. Sections 4.1.1 through 4.1.3 describe several recommended preparatory measures, including building and maintaining malware-related skills within the incident response team, facilitating communication and coordination throughout the organization, and acquiring necessary tools and resources.

4.1.1 Building and Maintaining Malware-Related Skills

In addition to standard incident response team skills, the following areas of knowledge may be of benefit for malware incident handlers:

- **Malware Infection Methods.** All malware incident handlers should have a solid understanding of how each major category of malware infects systems and spreads.

- **Malware Detection Tools.** As described in Section 3.4, malware can be detected by antivirus software, network-based and host-based intrusion prevention software, spyware detection and removal utilities, and other types of tools. Incident handlers who are familiar with the organization's implementations and configurations of malware detection tools should be better able to analyze supporting data and identify the characteristics of threats. All handlers should be familiar with the organization's antivirus software, at a minimum.

- **Computer Forensics.** Organizations should have at least a few incident handlers who are proficient with computer forensics tools and techniques. This expertise is needed when investigating the most challenging malware situations, such as suspected rootkit installations.[32]

- **Broad Understanding of IT.** This understanding allows handlers to assess the potential and likely impact of a malware threat across an organization and to make sound recommendations for containment, eradication, and recovery.

- **Programming.** Having team members with programming skills in popular scripting and macro languages, or relying on others within the organization who have programming expertise, can help the team understand the behavior and the potential impact of a new interpreted virus or worm in a matter of minutes.

Besides conducting malware-related training and exercises (as discussed in Section 4.1), organizations should also seek other ways of building and maintaining skills. One possibility is to have incident handlers temporarily work as antivirus engineers or administrators so that they can gain new technical skills and become more familiar with antivirus staff procedures and practices. Incident handlers could also work on a vulnerability management team temporarily to increase their knowledge of how vulnerable

---

[32] For more information on computer forensics, see NIST SP 800-86 (DRAFT), *Guide to Applying Forensic Techniques to Incident Response*, which is available at http://csrc.nist.gov/publications/nistpubs/.

systems are detected and patched; this exposure could help handlers make better containment and eradication decisions.

4.1.2 Facilitating Communication and Coordination

One of the most common problems during malware incident handling, particularly in widespread incidents, is poor communication and coordination. Anyone involved in an incident, including users, can inadvertently cause additional problems because of a limited view or understanding of the situation. To improve communication and coordination, an organization should designate in advance a few individuals or a small team to be responsible for coordinating the organization's responses to malware incidents. The coordinator's primary goal is to maintain situational awareness by gathering all pertinent information, making decisions that are in the best interests of the organization, and communicating pertinent information and decisions to all relevant parties within the organization in a timely manner. For malware incidents, the relevant parties often include end users, who might be given instructions on how to avoid infecting their systems, how to recognize the signs of an infection, and what to do if a system appears to be infected. The coordinator also needs to provide technical guidance and instructions to all staff assisting with containment, eradication, and recovery efforts, as well as giving management regular updates on the status of the response and the current and likely future impact of the incident.

Because widespread malware incidents often disrupt e-mail services, internal Web sites, Voice over IP, and other forms of communication, organizations should have several communication mechanisms established so that good communication and coordination among incident handlers, technical staff, management, and users can be sustained during adverse events. Possible communication methods include the organization's phone system, cell phones, pagers, e-mail, fax, and paper. Even under good conditions, it is often effective to use different communication methods for different audiences (for example, communicating to users through e-mail, but using a standard conference call phone number for discussions among key technical personnel). Management updates could occur in person, through conference calls, or through a voice mailbox greeting that is updated regularly with the incident status and other helpful information. Section 4.3.1 describes other methods for communicating with users, including sending broadcast voice mail messages and posting signs in high-traffic office areas.

Organizations should also establish a point of contact for answering questions about the legitimacy of malware alerts. Many organizations use the IT help desk as the initial point of contact and give help desk agents access to sources of information on real malware threats and virus hoaxes so that they can quickly determine the legitimacy of an alert and provide users with guidance on what to do.[33] Organizations should caution users not to forward malware alerts to others without first confirming that the alerts are legitimate.

4.1.3 Acquiring Tools and Resources

Organizations should also ensure that they have the necessary tools (hardware and software) and resources to assist in malware incident handling. Examples of tools include packet sniffers and protocol analyzers. Section 3.4 describes several additional tools such as antivirus software, spyware detection and removal utilities, and host-based IPS software that incident handlers should be able to use. Incident handling teams may choose to build hash sets of known good operating system and application files so that they are better prepared to determine how malware has altered a system.[34] Examples of resources

---

[33] Resources that can be helpful for determining the legitimacy of virus alerts include the Computer Incident Advisory Capability (CIAC) (http://ciac.llnl.gov/ciac/), the Computer Virus Myths site (http://www.vmyths.com/), and major antivirus manufacturers' Web sites.

[34] NIST's National Software Reference Library (NSRL) has hashes for files from many operating systems and applications. Handlers can also create hashes of files periodically. Handlers should rely on standard hash sets such as those from the

GUIDE TO MALWARE INCIDENT PREVENTION AND HANDLING

include lists of contact and on-call information, commonly used port numbers, and known critical assets. Table 4-1 provides a checklist of key tools and resources for malware incident handlers:[35]

Table 4-1. Tools and Resources for Malware Incident Handlers

Acquired	Tool / Resource
Malware Incident Handler Communications and Facilities	
	Contact information (e.g., phone numbers, e-mail addresses) for team members and others within and outside the organization (primary and backup contacts) who may have helpful information, such as antivirus vendors and other incident response teams
	On-call information for other teams within the organization, including escalation information
	Pagers or cell phones to be carried by team members for off-hour support, onsite communications
	Alternate Internet access method for finding information about new threats, downloading patches and updates, and reaching other Internet-based resources when Internet access is lost during a severe malware incident
	War room for central communication and coordination; if a permanent war room is not necessary, the team should create a procedure for procuring a temporary war room when needed
Malware Incident Analysis Hardware and Software	
	Laptops, which provide easily portable workstations for activities such as analyzing data and sniffing packets
	Spare workstations, servers, and networking equipment, which may be used for trying out malware in an isolated environment; if the team cannot justify the expense of additional equipment, perhaps equipment in an existing test lab could be used, or a virtual lab could be established using OS emulation software
	Blank media, such as floppy diskettes and CDs, for storing and transporting malware samples and other files as needed
	Packet sniffers and protocol analyzers to capture and analyze network traffic that may contain malware activity
	Up-to-date, trusted versions of OS executables and analysis utilities, stored on floppy diskettes or CDs, to be used to examine systems for signs of malware infection (e.g., antivirus software, spyware detection and removal utilities, system administration tools, forensics utilities)
Malware Incident Analysis Resources	
	Port lists, including commonly used ports and known Trojan horse and backdoor ports
	Documentation for OSs, applications, protocols, and antivirus and intrusion detection signatures
	Network diagrams and lists of critical assets, such as Web, e-mail, and File Transfer Protocol (FTP) servers
	Baselines of expected network, system and application activity
Malware Incident Mitigation Software	
	Media, including OS boot disks and CDs, OS media, and application media
	Security patches from OS and application vendors
	Disk imaging software and backup images of OS, applications, and data stored on secondary media

---

NSRL project whenever possible, and create custom hash sets primarily for organization-specific files. Because Federal agencies must use FIPS-approved encryption algorithms contained in validated cryptographic modules, handlers should use SHA-1 instead of MD5 for file hashes whenever possible.

[35] Additional resources are listed in Appendix F.

4.2 Detection

Organizations should strive to detect and validate malware incidents rapidly, because infections can spread through an organization in a matter of minutes. Early detection can help the organization minimize the number of infected systems, which should lessen the magnitude of the recovery effort and the amount of damage the organization sustains. Although major incidents might hit an organization so quickly that there is no time for anyone to react, most incidents occur more slowly.

Because malware can take many forms and be distributed through many means, there are many possible signs of a malware incident and many locations within an organization where the signs might be recorded or observed. It sometimes takes considerable analysis, requiring extensive technical knowledge and experience, to confirm that an incident has been caused by malware, particularly if the malware threat is new and unknown. After malware incident detection and validation, incident handlers should determine the type, extent, and magnitude of the problem as quickly as possible so that the response to the incident can be given the appropriate priority. Sections 4.2.1 through 4.2.3 provide guidance on understanding the signs of malware incidents, identifying the characteristics of incidents, and determining incident scope and prioritizing response efforts.

4.2.1 Understanding Signs of Malware Incidents

Signs of a malware incident fall into two categories: precursors and indications. A *precursor* is a sign that a malware attack may occur in the future. An *indication* is a sign that a malware incident may have occurred or may be occurring.

Most malware precursors take one of the following forms:

- **Malware Advisories.** Antivirus vendors and other security-related organizations distribute and post advisories concerning major new malware threats. Incident handlers should subscribe to malware advisory mailing lists so that they receive advance warning of threats that could affect the organization in the coming hours or days. Incident handlers might also hear reports of new malware from general security mailing lists, as well as from peers at other organizations that have already been affected. In addition, organizations can pay for early warning services that identify and analyze emerging malware threats, with the intent of providing reliable information to service subscribers before the information is publicly available from other sources, such as antivirus vendors.

- **Security Tool Alerts.** Tools such as antivirus software and IPSs can detect and quarantine, delete, or otherwise prevent instances of malware from infecting systems. These actions cause security tool alerts to be generated, which might be signs of a subsequent incident. For example, after malware attempts but fails to enter a system through one means (resulting in alerts), the same type of malware could enter the organization through an unmonitored attack vector (e.g., an unsecured modem) or reach a system that had not been properly secured, causing an incident.

Detecting precursors gives organizations an opportunity to prevent incidents by altering their security posture and to be on the alert to handle incidents that occur shortly after the precursor. In the most serious cases, if it seems nearly certain that the organization is about to experience a major incident, organizations might decide to act as if the incident were already occurring and begin to mobilize their incident response capabilities. Nevertheless, many, if not most, malware incidents do not have clear precursors, and precursors often appear immediately before an incident; therefore, organizations should not rely on such advance warning.

Although incidents frequently occur without clear precursors, there are often many indications that a malware incident is underway. Examples of indications are as follows:

■ A Web server crashes.

■ Users complain of slow access to hosts on the Internet, exhaustion of system resources, slow disk access, or slow system boots.

■ Antivirus software detects that a host is infected with a worm and generates an alert.

■ A system administrator sees a filename with unusual characters.

■ A host records an auditing configuration change in its log.

■ Whenever a user tries to run a Web browser, the user's laptop reboots itself.

■ An e-mail administrator sees a large number of bounced e-mails with suspicious content.

■ Security controls such as antivirus software and personal firewalls are disabled on many hosts.

■ A network administrator notices an unusual deviation from typical network traffic flows.

Most of these indications could have causes other than malware. For example, a Web server could crash because of a non-malware attack, an OS flaw, or a power disruption, among other reasons. Bounced e-mails could be caused by a system hardware failure or e-mail server misconfiguration, or they might be spoofed by a spammer. These complications illustrate the challenges involved in detecting and validating a malware incident, and the need to have well-trained, technically knowledgeable incident handlers who can perform analysis quickly to determine what has happened. Handlers should be adept at reviewing possible indications from many different sources and correlating data among the sources to identify malware-related activity. The primary sources of indications fall into a few broad categories:

■ **Users.** Users often report malware-related indications to the help desk and other technical support staff. For example, users might see antivirus alerts on their workstations, experience operational failures, or notice unusual behavior. Users may also be the cause of an infection and may call the help desk after inadvertently doing something they should not have.

■ **IT Staff.** System, network, and security administrators, as well as other IT staff members, usually are familiar with normal activity and are sensitive to observed significant deviations from expected behavior.

■ **Security Tools.** Some security tools, such as antivirus software and IPSs, may record explicit indications of malware. Other tools, such as network monitoring software, may report deviations from expected behavior without specifically labeling it as malware related. The alerts and other information produced by security tools need to be monitored frequently or continuously to be of value in detecting malware.

The variety of characteristics exhibited by malware is so great that it is not feasible to develop a comprehensive list of indications. However, Table 4-2 lists the most likely indications of a malware incident for various types of malware and attacker tools. This table may help individuals identify and classify possible malware incidents more quickly. Indications for incidents in which malware has achieved administrator-level access are not represented in Table 4-2. If malware achieves this level of access on a system, it may be able to perform virtually any possible action on the system. Accordingly, the indications for such incidents are nearly endless.

Table 4-2. Likely Malware Indications

Indication	Malware Type						Attacker Tool Type				
	Multipartite Virus	Macro Virus	Network Service Worm	Mass Mailing Worm	Trojan Horse	Malicious Mobile Code	Backdoor[36]	Keystroke Logger	Rootkit	Malicious Browser Plug-Ins	E-mail Generators
Security Tools											
Antivirus software alerts	✓	✓	✓	✓	✓	✓	✓	✓	✓	✓	✓
Spyware detection and removal utility alerts					✓	✓				✓	
Network-based intrusion prevention alerts			✓	✓			✓				
Host-based intrusion detection alerts for changes to files					✓				✓		
Firewall and router log entries			✓				✓				
Observed Host Activity											
System cannot boot	✓								✓		
Error message displayed during system boot	✓								✓		
System instability and crashes occur		✓	✓		✓		✓		✓		
Programs start slowly, run slowly, or do not run at all	✓	✓	✓		✓				✓	✓	
Unknown processes are run at system startup					✓		✓	✓			✓
Unusual and unexpected ports open							✓				
Sudden increase occurs in the number of e-mails being sent and received		✓		✓					✓		
Changes are made in templates for word processing documents, spreadsheets, etc.		✓									
Web browser configuration is changed, such as different home page and new toolbars						✓				✓	
Files are deleted, corrupted, or inaccessible	✓	✓			✓				✓		
Unusual items appear on the screen, such as odd messages, graphics, and overlapping or overlaid message boxes		✓				✓			✓		✓
Unexpected dialog boxes appear, requesting permission to do something						✓				✓	
Observed Network Activity											
Significantly increased network usage			✓	✓			✓				✓
Port scans and failed connection attempts targeted at the vulnerable service (e.g., open Windows shares, HTTP)			✓				✓				
Network connections between the host and unknown remote systems			✓		✓	✓	✓	✓	✓	✓	✓

---

36   This category includes bots and remote administration tools.

4.2.2 Identifying Malware Incident Characteristics

Because no indication is completely reliable—even antivirus software might miscategorize benign activity as malicious—incident handlers need to analyze any suspected malware incident and validate that malware is the cause. In some cases, such as a massive, organization-wide infection, validation may be unnecessary because the nature of the incident is obvious. The goal is for incident handlers to be as certain as feasible that an incident is caused by malware and to have a basic understanding of the type of malware threat responsible, such as a worm or a Trojan horse. If the source of the incident cannot easily be confirmed, it is often better to respond as if it were caused by malware and to alter response efforts if it is later determined that malware is not involved. Waiting for conclusive evidence of malware might have a serious negative impact on response efforts and significantly increase the damage sustained by the organization.

As part of the analysis and validation process, incident handlers typically identify characteristics of the malware activity by examining detection sources. Understanding the activity's characteristics is very helpful in assigning an appropriate priority to the incident response efforts and planning effective containment, eradication, and recovery activities. Incident handlers should collaborate with security administrators in advance to identify data sources that can aid in detecting malware information and to understand what types of information each data source may record. In addition to the obvious sources of data, such as antivirus software, incident handlers should be aware of and use secondary sources, including the following:

- Firewall and router log files, which might show blocked connection attempts

- Log files from e-mail servers and network-based IPS sensors, which might record e-mail headers or attachment names

- Packet capture files from packet sniffers, network-based IPS sensors, and network forensic analysis tools, which might contain a recording of malware-related network traffic.

Once incident handlers have reviewed detection source data and identified a few characteristics of the malware, the handlers should be able to search for those characteristics in antivirus vendors' malware databases and identify which instance of malware is the most likely cause. If the malware has been known for some time, it is likely that antivirus vendors will have a substantial amount of information on it, such as the following:

- Malware category (e.g., virus, worm, Trojan horse)

- Services and ports that are attacked

- Vulnerabilities that are exploited

- E-mail subjects, attachment names, attachment sizes, body content

- Which versions of operating systems, devices, applications, etc., may be affected

- How the malware infects the system (e.g., vulnerability, misconfiguration)

- How the malware affects the infected system, including the names and locations of affected files, altered configuration settings, installed backdoor ports, etc.

- How the malware propagates and how to approach containment

- How to remove the malware from the system.

Unfortunately, the newest threats might not be included in malware databases for several hours or days, depending on the relative importance of the threat. Therefore, incident handlers might need to consult other sources of information so that response efforts can begin sooner. One option is using public security mailing lists, which might contain first-hand accounts of malware incidents; however, such reports are often incomplete or inaccurate, so incident handlers should validate any information obtained from these sources. Another potentially valuable source of malware characteristic information is peers at other organizations. If a major new threat is spreading relatively slowly around the world, other organizations may have already been affected and gathered data on the threat. For example, an e-mail–borne virus might affect organizations in the eastern United States sooner than it affects those in the western United States if the virus started spreading at 6 a.m. Eastern time on a weekday. Establishing and maintaining good relationships with peers at other organizations that face similar problems can be advantageous for all involved.

Incident handlers can also study the behavior of malware on a regular system that has been infected or on a malware test system. For example, an incident handler could acquire a malware sample from an infected system and place the malware on an isolated test system. An infected system, or a disk image of an infected system, could also be placed into an isolated test environment. The test environment should include suites of tools for collecting information about malware, such as packet sniffers to record network activity and file integrity checkers to detect file modifications on the test system. Malware test systems and environments are helpful not only for analyzing current malware threats without the risk of inadvertently causing additional damage to the organization, but also for training staff in malware incident handling.

To assist in analyzing the behavior of malware on a system, analysts should construct trusted toolkits on removable media.[37] A toolkit should contain up-to-date tools for identifying malware (e.g., antivirus software, spyware detection and removal utilities), listing the currently running processes, and displaying network connections, as well as other potentially helpful utilities. The toolkit media should be protected from alteration or infection by malware; for example, floppy disks should be write-protected, and CD sessions should be finalized, which ensures that no additional data can be written to the CDs. The motivation for using such a trusted toolkit is that malware on the system may have disabled or altered the functionality of the security tools on the system itself, such as antivirus software, so that they do not report malicious activity. By running tools from a protected, verified toolkit, incident handlers can gain a more accurate understanding of the activity on the system.

4.2.3 Prioritizing Incident Response

Once a malware incident has been validated, the next activity is to prioritize its handling. Certain forms of malware, such as worms, tend to spread very quickly and can cause a substantial impact in minutes or hours, so they often necessitate a high-priority response. Other forms of malware, such as Trojan horses, tend to affect a single system; the response to such incidents should be based on the value of the data and services provided by the system. Organizations should establish a set of criteria that identify the appropriate level of response for various malware-related situations. The criteria should incorporate considerations such as the following:

- How the malware entered the environment and what transmission mechanisms it uses

---

[37] One option for creating a trusted toolkit is to use an existing LiveCD, which is a CD containing a bootable operating system. By booting a system with a LiveCD, an analyst can examine the system's contents without booting the system's own operating system. LiveCDs exist for many versions of different operating systems.

- What type of malware it is (e.g., virus, worm, Trojan horse)

- Which types of attacker tools are placed onto the system by the malware

- What networks and systems the malware is affecting and how it is affecting them

- How the impact of the incident is likely to increase in the following minutes, hours, and days if the incident is not contained.

4.3 Containment

Containment of malware has two major components: stopping the spread of the malware and preventing further damage to systems. Nearly every malware incident requires containment actions. In addressing an incident, it is important for an organization to decide which methods of containment to employ initially, early in the response. Containment of isolated incidents and incidents involving noninfectious forms of malware is generally straightforward, involving such actions as disconnecting the affected systems from networks or shutting down the systems. For more widespread malware incidents, organizations should use a strategy that contains the incident for most systems as quickly as possible; this should limit the number of machines that are infected, the amount of damage that is done, and the amount of time that it will take to fully recover all data and services.

In containing a malware incident, it is also important to understand that stopping the spread of malware does not necessarily prevent all further damage to systems. Even after an organization has stopped its spread, malware on a system might continue to infect or delete data, application, and OS files. In addition, some instances of malware are designed to cause additional damage when network connectivity is lost or other containment measures are performed. For example, an infected system might run a malicious process that contacts another system periodically. If that connectivity is lost because the infected system is disconnected from the network, the malware might overwrite all the data on the host's hard drive. For these reasons, handlers should not assume that just because a host has been disconnected from the network, further damage to the host has been prevented, and in many cases, should begin eradication efforts as soon as possible to prevent more damage.

Organizations should have strategies and procedures in place for making containment-related decisions that reflect the level of risk acceptable to the organization. For example, an organization might decide that infected systems performing critical functions should not be disconnected from networks or shut down if the likely damage to the organization from those functions being unavailable would be greater than the security risks posed by not isolating or shutting down the system. Containment strategies should support incident handlers in selecting the appropriate combination of containment methods based on the characteristics of a particular situation.

Containment methods can be divided into four basic categories: relying on user participation, performing automated detection, temporarily halting services, and blocking certain types of network connectivity. Sections 4.3.1 through 4.3.4 describe each category in detail.

4.3.1 Containment Through User Participation

User participation, particularly during large-scale incidents, can be a valuable part of containment efforts. Users can be provided with instructions on how to identify infections and what measures to take if a system is infected, such as calling the help desk, disconnecting the system from the network, or powering off the system. The instructions might also cover malware eradication, such as updating antivirus signatures and performing a system scan, or obtaining and running a specialized malware eradication utility. Having users perform such actions is particularly helpful in non-managed environments and other situations in which use of fully automated containment methods (such as those described in Sections 4.3.2 through 4.3.4) is not feasible.

As described in Section 4.1.2, effectively communicating helpful information to users in a timely manner is challenging. Although e-mail is typically the most efficient communication mechanism, it might be unavailable during major incidents, or users might not read the e-mail until it is too late. Therefore, organizations should have several alternate mechanisms in place for distributing information to users, such as sending messages to all voice mailboxes within the organization, posting signs in work areas, and handing out instructions at building and office entrances. Displaying a system message at login might be somewhat effective, but many users do not log out for days or weeks at a time, and many users also tend to ignore such messages. Organizations with significant numbers of users in alternate locations, such as home offices and small branch offices, should ensure that the communication mechanisms reach these users. Another important consideration is that users might need to be provided with software, such as cleanup utilities, and software updates, such as patches and updated antivirus signatures. Organizations should identify and implement multiple methods for delivering software utilities and updates to users who are expected to assist with containment.

Although user participation can be very helpful for containment, organizations should not rely primarily on this means for containing malware incidents. No matter how containment guidance is communicated, it is unlikely that all users will receive it and realize that it might pertain to them. In addition, some users who receive containment instructions are unlikely to follow the directions successfully because of a lack of understanding, a simple mistake in following the directions, or system-specific characteristics that make the directions incorrect for that system. Some users also might be focused on performing their regular tasks and be unconcerned about the possible effects of malware on their systems. Nevertheless, for large-scale incidents involving a sizable percentage of the organization's systems, user involvement in containment can significantly reduce the burden on incident handlers and technical support staff in responding to the incident.

4.3.2 Containment Through Automated Detection

Many malware incidents can be contained primarily through the use of the automated technologies described in Section 3.4 for preventing and detecting infections. These technologies include antivirus software, e-mail filtering, and intrusion prevention software. Because antivirus software on hosts can detect and remove infections, it is often the preferred automated detection method for assisting in containment. Detection tools that were not capable of recognizing or stopping malware when it was a new threat can usually be updated or reconfigured to recognize the same malware's characteristics later and stop it from spreading. Unfortunately, doing so in a timely manner during a major incident can be a difficult undertaking. For example, it might not be feasible to distribute software updates using networks and systems (e.g., antivirus servers) that have already been seriously impaired by the volume of malware activity, particularly if updates need to be distributed to many or most hosts within the organization as quickly as possible. Although this type of problem can be mitigated somewhat by reserving network bandwidth for software updates and creating robust distributed infrastructures for automated detection technologies, some malware threats are so severe that they may disrupt most network communications temporarily. Moreover, even if updates can be distributed, it is usually not possible to update all systems immediately. For example, some systems might not have antivirus software enabled or configured correctly. This last obstacle is especially characteristic of non-managed environments, in which users tend to have greater control over their systems; however, some malware disables antivirus software and other security controls, so even in managed environments, it may not be possible to update a significant percentage of systems automatically.

In a widespread incident, if malware cannot be identified by updated antivirus software, or updated signatures are not yet fully deployed, organizations should be prepared to use other security tools to contain the malware until the antivirus signatures can perform the containment effectively.[38] After an organization receives updated signatures, it is prudent to test them at least minimally before deployment, to ensure that the update itself should not cause a negative impact on the organization. Another reason to use multiple security tools for automated detection and containment activities is load balancing. Expecting antivirus software to handle the complete workload of a malware incident is unrealistic during high-volume infections. By using a defense-in-depth strategy for detecting and blocking malware, an organization can spread the workload across multiple components. A further benefit of having multiple types of automated detection ready is that different detectors may be more effective in different situations. Examples of automated detection methods other than antivirus software are as follows:

- **E-mail Filtering.** E-mail servers and clients, as well as anti-spam software, can be configured to block e-mails or e-mail attachments that have certain characteristics, such as a known bad subject, sender, message text, or attachment name or type.[39] However, malware increasingly uses a wider variety of characteristics; for example, a virus could use a hundred different subjects, any of which could also be used for legitimate e-mails. Some viruses even generate random subjects or attachment names, or create replies to existing benign e-mails, which might render e-mail filtering methods useless. In addition, although most malicious file attachments have suspicious file extensions (particularly *.bat, .cmd, .exe, .pif,* and *.scr)*, the use of once-benign file extensions, such as *.zip,* has become more prevalent for malicious file attachments.

- **Network-Based IPS Software.** Most IPS products allow their prevention capabilities to be enabled for specific signatures. If a network-based IPS device is inline, meaning that it is an active part of the network, and it has a signature for the malware, it should be able to identify the malware and stop it from reaching its targets. If the IPS device does not have its prevention capabilities enabled, it may be prudent during a severe incident to reconfigure or redeploy one or more IPS sensors and enable IPS so they can stop the activity. IPS technologies should be able to stop both incoming and outgoing infection attempts. Of course, the value of IPSs in malware containment depends on the availability and accuracy of a signature to identify the malware. Several IPS products allow administrators to write custom signatures based on some of the known characteristics of the malware, or to customize existing signatures. For example, an IPS may allow administrators to specify known bad e-mail attachment names or subjects, or to specify known bad destination port numbers. In many cases, IPS administrators can have their own accurate signature in place hours before antivirus vendors have signatures available. In addition, because the IPS signature affects only network-based IPS sensors, whereas antivirus signatures generally affect all workstations and servers, it is generally less risky to rapidly deploy a new IPS signature than new antivirus signatures.

- **Host-Based IPS Software.** Some host-based IPS products can restrict certain executables from being run. For example, administrators can enter the names of files that should not be executed. If antivirus signatures are not yet available for a new threat, it might be possible to configure host-based IPS software to block the execution of the files that are part of the new threat.

[38] Incident handlers should also be familiar with the organization's policy and procedures for submitting copies of unknown malware to the organization's antivirus vendors and other security software vendors for analysis. This practice can help vendors respond more quickly to new threats. Organizations should also contact trusted parties, such as incident response organizations and antivirus vendors, when needed and as permitted by the organization's policy, for guidance on handling new threats.
[39] Generally, it is feasible only in highly managed environments to configure e-mail clients throughout the organization to block certain e-mails or e-mail attachments.

4.3.3 Containment through Disabling Services

Some malware incidents necessitate more drastic and potentially disruptive measures for containment. For example, an incident might generate so much network traffic or application activity, such as e-mails or file transfers that many applications could effectively be made unavailable. Containing such an incident quickly and effectively might be accomplished through a loss of services, such as shutting down a service used by malware, blocking a certain service at the network perimeter, or disabling portions of a service (e.g., large mailing lists). Also, a service might provide a channel for infection or for transferring data from infected hosts. In either case, shutting down the affected services might be the best way to contain the infection without losing all services. This action is typically performed at the application level (e.g., disabling a service on servers) or at the network level (e.g., configuring firewalls to block IP addresses or ports associated with a service). The goal is to disable as little functionality as possible while containing the incident effectively. To support the disabling of network services, organizations should maintain lists of the services they use and the TCP and UDP ports used by each service.

The service most commonly affected by malware is e-mail. E-mail servers can become completely overwhelmed by viruses or worms trying to spread via e-mail. Shutting down e-mail servers to halt the spread of e-mail–borne malware can largely contain some incidents very quickly. However, in some cases, an organization might have unknown e-mail servers (e.g., a file server inadvertently running an e-mail server) that also need to be shut down, which could slow containment. In less severe circumstances, disabling portions of e-mail services might provide effective containment without causing the loss of all e-mail services. For example, temporarily disabling unmoderated mailing lists might significantly reduce the spread of malware and the strain on e-mail servers.

From a technology standpoint, disabling a service is generally a simple process; understanding the consequences of doing so tends to be more challenging. Disabling a service that the organization relies on has an obvious negative impact on the organization's functions. Also, disabling a service might inadvertently disrupt other services that depend on it. For example, disabling e-mail services could impair directory services that replicate information through e-mail. Organizations should maintain a list of dependencies between major services so that incident handlers are aware of them when making containment decisions. Also, organizations might find it helpful to provide alternative services with similar functionality. For example, in a highly managed environment, if a vulnerability in an e-mail client were being exploited by a new virus, users could be blocked temporarily from using that e-mail client and instead directed to use a Web-based e-mail client that did not have the vulnerability. This step would help contain the incident while providing users with e-mail access. The same strategy could be used for cases involving exploitation of vulnerabilities in Web browsers and other common client applications.

Organizations should also be prepared to respond to problems caused by other organizations disabling their own services in response to a malware incident. For example, an organization that has a team temporarily working for another organization might have configured the team members' e-mail accounts to forward their e-mail to accounts on the other organization's e-mail system. In this case, if the other organization disabled e-mail services, forwarded e-mails might be bounced back, then reforwarded, then bounced again, resulting in a mail loop. If this happened, a handful of user accounts could cause a significant degradation in e-mail services.

4.3.4 Containment through Disabling Connectivity

Containing incidents by placing temporary restrictions on network connectivity can be very effective. For example, if infected systems attempt to establish connections with any one of several external systems to download rootkits, handlers should consider blocking all access to the external systems' IP addresses. Similarly, if infected systems within the organization attempt to spread their malware, the organization might block network traffic from the systems' IP addresses to control the situation while the infected hosts are physically located and disinfected. An alternative to blocking network access for particular IP addresses is to disconnect the infected systems from the network, which could be accomplished by reconfiguring network devices to deny network access or physically disconnecting network cables or ejecting removable network interface cards from infected systems.

The most drastic containment step is purposely breaking needed network connectivity for uninfected systems. This could eliminate network access for groups of systems, such as remote dial-in and VPN users. In worst-case scenarios, isolating subnets from the primary network or even disconnecting the entire organization from the Internet might be necessary to stop the spread of malware, halt damage to systems, and provide an opportunity to mitigate vulnerabilities. Implementing a widespread loss of connectivity to achieve containment is most likely to be acceptable to an organization in cases in which malware activity is already causing severe network disruptions or infected systems are performing an attack against other organizations. Because a major loss of connectivity almost always affects many organizational functions, connectivity usually must be restored as soon as possible.

Organizations can design and implement their networks to make containment through loss of connectivity easier to do and less disruptive. For example, some organizations place their servers and workstations on separate subnets; during a malware incident targeting workstations, the infected workstation subnets can be isolated from the main network, and the server subnets can continue to provide functionality to external customers and internal workstation subnets that are not infected. Another network design strategy related to malware containment is the use of separate virtual local area networks (VLAN) for infected systems. With this design, a host's security posture is checked when it wants to join the network. This is often done by placing on each host an agent that monitors various characteristics of the host, such as OS patches and antivirus updates. When the host attempts to connect to the network, a network device such as a router requests information from the host's agent. If the host does not respond to the request or the response indicates that the host is insecure, the network device causes the host to be placed onto a separate VLAN. The same technique can be used with hosts that are already on the organization's regular networks, allowing infected hosts to be moved automatically to a separate VLAN.[40]

Having a separate VLAN for infected hosts also helps organizations to provide antivirus signature updates and OS and application patches to the hosts while severely restricting what they can do. Without a separate VLAN, the organization might need to remove infected hosts' network access entirely, which necessitates transferring and applying updates manually to each host to contain and eradicate the malware and mitigate vulnerabilities. A variant of the separate VLAN strategy that can be effective in some situations is to place all hosts on a particular network segment in a VLAN and then move hosts to the production network as each is deemed to be clean and patched. One drawback of using a VLAN is that the traffic from the infected hosts is still carried through the same devices as the production traffic; it provides logical separation but not physical. As a result, large volumes of traffic on the VLAN, produced by malware-generated activity and system updating and patching, could cause operational problems for all users of the network devices.

4.3.5 Containment Recommendations

Containment can be performed through many methods in the four categories described above (users, automated detection, loss of services, and loss of connectivity). Because no single malware containment category or individual method is appropriate or effective in every situation, incident handlers should select a combination of containment methods that is likely to be effective in containing the current

---

[40] Microsoft has developed a platform for this called Network Access Protection (NAP). More information on NAP is available at http://www.microsoft.com/windowsserver2003/technologies/networking/nap/default.mspx.

incident while limiting damage to systems and reducing the impact that containment methods might have on other systems. For example, shutting down all network access might be very effective at stopping the spread of malware, but it would also allow infections on systems to continue damaging files and would disrupt many important functions of the organization.

The most drastic containment methods can be tolerated by most organizations for only a brief period of time. Accordingly, organizations should support sound containment decisions by having policies that clearly state who has authority to make major containment decisions and under what circumstances various actions (e.g., disconnecting the organization from the Internet) are appropriate.

4.3.6   Identification of Infected Hosts

Identifying hosts that are infected by malware is part of every malware incident, and particularly important for widespread incidents. Once identified, infected hosts can undergo the appropriate containment, eradication, and recovery actions. Unfortunately, identifying infected hosts is often complicated by the dynamic nature of computing. For instance, people shut systems down, disconnect them from networks, or move them from place to place, making it extremely difficult to identify which hosts are currently infected. In addition, some hosts can boot to multiple OSs or use virtual operating system software; an infection in one OS instantiation might not be detectable when a system is currently using another OS.

Accurate identification of infected hosts can also be complicated by other factors. For example, systems with unmitigated vulnerabilities might be disinfected and reinfected multiple times. Some instances of malware actually remove some or all traces of other malware, which could cause the partially or fully removed infections to go undetected. Identifying all hosts involved in large-scale incidents is often particularly challenging because of the sheer number of infected systems. In addition, the data concerning infected hosts might come from several sources—antivirus software, IDSs, user reports, and other methods—and be very difficult to consolidate and keep current.

Ideally, all identification could be performed through automated means, but for various reasons (described in Sections 4.3.6.1 and 4.3.6.2), this is usually not possible. Manual identification methods, such as relying on users to identify and report infected systems, and having technical staff personally check each system, are not feasible for comprehensive identification during incidents in most organizations. Organizations should carefully consider host identification issues before a large-scale malware incident occurs so that they are prepared to use multiple identification strategies as part of implementing effective containment strategies. Organizations should also determine which types of identifying information might be needed and what data sources might record the information. For example, a host's current IP address is typically needed for remote actions; of course, a host's physical location is needed for local actions. One piece of information can often be used to determine others, such as mapping an IP address to a media access control (MAC) address, which could then be mapped to a switch serving a particular group of offices. If an IP address can be mapped to a system owner or user— for example, by recording the mapping during network login—the owner or user can be contacted to provide the host's location.

The difficulty in identifying the physical location of an infected host depends on several factors. In a managed environment, identifying a host's location is often relatively easy because of the standardized manner in which things are done. For example, system names might contain the user's ID or office number, or the system's serial number (which can be tied to a user ID). Also, asset inventory management tools might contain current information on host characteristics. In other environments, especially those in which users have full control over their systems and network management is not centralized, it might be challenging to link a machine to a location. For example, an administrator might know that the system at address 10.3.1.70 appears to be infected but not have any idea where that machine resides or who uses it. Administrators might need to track down an infected system through network devices. For example, a switch port mapper can poll switches for a particular IP address and identify the switch port number and host name associated with that IP address. If the infected system is several switches away, it can take hours to track down a single machine; if the infected system is not directly switched, the administrator might still need to manually trace connectivity through various wiring closets and network devices. An alternative is to pull the network cable or shut down the switch port for an apparently infected system and wait for a user to report an outage. This approach can inadvertently cause a loss of connectivity for small numbers of uninfected systems, but if performed carefully as a last-resort identification and containment method, it can be quite effective.

Some organizations first make reasonable efforts to identify infected hosts and perform containment, eradication, and recovery efforts on them, then implement measures to prevent hosts that have not been verified as uninfected and properly secured from attaching to the network. These measures should be discussed well in advance, and incident handlers should have prior written permission to lock out hosts under certain circumstances. Generally, lockout measures are based on the characteristics of particular hosts, such as MAC addresses or static IP addresses, but lockouts can also be performed based on user ID if a system is associated with a single user. Another possibility is to use network login scripts to identify and deny access to infected hosts, but this might be ineffective if an infected system starts spreading malware after system boot but before user authentication. As described in Section 4.3.4, having a separate VLAN for infected or unverified hosts can provide a good way to lock out systems, as long as the mechanism to detect infections is reliable. Although lockout methods might be needed only under extreme circumstances, organizations should think in advance about how individual hosts or users could be locked out so that if needed, lockouts can be performed rapidly.

Sections 4.3.6.1 through 4.3.6.3 discuss the possible categories of infected host identification techniques: forensic, active, and manual.

4.3.6.1 Forensic Identification

Forensic identification is the practice of identifying infected systems by looking for evidence of recent infections. The evidence may be very recent (only a few minutes old) or not so recent (hours or days old); the older the information is, the less accurate it is likely to be. The most obvious sources of evidence are those that are designed to identify malware activity, such as antivirus software, spyware detection and removal utilities, content filtering (e.g., anti-spam measures), and host-based intrusion prevention software. The logs of security applications might contain detailed records of suspicious activity, and might also indicate whether a security compromise occurred or was prevented. If the security application is part of a managed enterprise deployment, logs might be available both on individual hosts and in a centralized application log.

In situations in which the typical sources of evidence do not contain the necessary information, organizations might need to turn to secondary sources, such as the following:

- **Network Device Logs.** Firewalls, routers, and other filtering devices that record connection activity, as well as network monitoring tools, might be helpful in identifying network connection activity (e.g., specific port number combinations, unusual protocols) consistent with certain malware.

- **Sinkhole Routers.** A *sinkhole router* is a router within an organization that receives all traffic that has an unknown route (e.g., destination IP addresses on an unused subnet). Malware attempting to propagate may generate such traffic; thus, unusual changes in the traffic seen by the sinkhole router could indicate a new malware threat. Establishing sinkhole routers that can capture all network traffic with unknown routes can be effective at identifying infected systems within an organization that are attempting to infect other systems. A sinkhole router is usually configured to send information about received traffic to a log server and an IDS; a packet sniffer is also used sometimes to record the suspicious activity.

- **Application Server Logs.** Applications commonly used as malware transmission mechanisms, such as e-mail and HTTP, might record information in their logs that indicates which hosts were infected. From end to end, information regarding a single e-mail message might be recorded in several places: the sender's system, each e-mail server that handles the message, and the recipient's system, as well as antivirus, spam, and content filtering servers. Similarly, hosts running Web browsers can provide a rich resource for information on malicious Web activity, including a list of favorite Web sites, a history of Web sites visited and the dates and times that they were visited, cached Web data files, and cookies (including their creation and expiration dates). Another helpful source of information is DNS server logs, which might show infected hosts attempting to get the IP address for an external malicious site that they wish to transfer data to or otherwise interact with.

- **Network Forensic Tools.** Software programs that capture and record packets, such as network forensic analysis tools and packet sniffers, might have highly detailed information on malware activity. However, because these tools record so much information about most or all network activity, it can be very time-intensive to extract just the needed information. More efficient means of identifying infected hosts are often available.

Using forensic data for identifying infected hosts can be advantageous over other methods because the data has already been collected—the pertinent data just needs to be extracted from the total data set. Unfortunately, for some data sources, extracting the data can take a considerable amount of time. Also, event information can become outdated quickly, causing uninfected hosts to undergo containment unnecessarily and allowing infected hosts to avoid containment measures. If an accurate, comprehensive, and reasonably current source of forensic data is available, it might provide the most effective way of identifying infected hosts.

4.3.6.2 Active Identification

Active identification methods are used to identify which hosts are currently infected. Immediately after identifying an infection, some active approaches can be used to perform containment and eradication measures for the host, such as running a disinfection utility, deploying patches or antivirus updates, or moving the host to a VLAN for infected systems. Active identification can be performed through several methods, including the following:

- **Login Script.** Network login scripts can typically be modified to check certain host characteristics for signs of malware. The disadvantage of identifying hosts through login scripts is that infected hosts might not leave and attempt to rejoin the network for days, weeks, or months after the infection occurs.

- **Custom Network-Based IPS or IDS Signature.** Writing a custom IPS or IDS signature that identifies infected hosts is often a highly effective technique. Some organizations have separate IPS or IDS sensors with strong signature-writing capabilities that can be dedicated to identifying malware infections. This provides a high-quality source of information while keeping other sensors from becoming overloaded with malware alerts.

- **Packet Sniffers.** Configuring packet sniffers to look only for network traffic matching the characteristics of a particular malware threat can be effective at identifying infected hosts. Packet sniffers are most helpful if most or all malware-generated network traffic attempts to pass through the same network device or a few devices.

- **Vulnerability Assessment Software.** Many software programs designed to identify host vulnerabilities can also detect certain known malware threats. However, vulnerability assessment software typically is not helpful in identifying hosts infected by a new threat. Also, many vulnerability assessment tools may be unable to detect vulnerabilties present on hosts that are using host-based firewalls.

- **Host Scans.** If a particular malware threat causes infected hosts to run a backdoor that listens at a particular port, a host scan for that port can be effective at finding infected hosts.

- **Other Scans.** In addition to host scans, other types of scans might also be helpful in finding hosts with certain characteristics, such as a particular configuration setting or a system file with a certain size that indicates an infection.

It is best to use a combination of active approaches because each individual approach is only helpful at finding certain types of infections on certain hosts. For example, host scans might be unsuccessful at identifying infections on hosts that are running personal firewalls, because the firewalls block the scans, but packet sniffers and login scripts might be able to identify the infections on those hosts. Although a combination of active approaches can produce highly accurate results, active approaches need to be used repeatedly because the status of infections changes constantly and the data is gathered over a period of time.

4.3.6.3 Manual Identification

Another method for identifying infected hosts is the manual approach. This is by far the most labor-intensive of the three methods, but it is often a necessary measure to successfully identify infected hosts. When networks are completely overwhelmed by infection-related traffic, active approaches may not be possible. When malware network traffic uses spoofed addresses and generates high volumes of activity, forensic approaches may not be practical because the valid entries may be lost in the enormous volume of data. Also, if users have control over their systems, as they do in many non-managed environments, the characteristics of systems may be so different that the results of automated identification methods are quite incomplete and inaccurate. In such situations, a primarily manual approach might be the best option.

There are a few possible techniques for implementing a manual approach. One is to ask users to identify infections themselves by providing them with information on the malware and the signs of an infection, as well as antivirus software, OS or application patches, or scanning tools. These items may need to be distributed on CDs or other media. A similar manual technique is to have local IT staffers (including individuals who normally do not participate in malware incident handling) either check all systems or check systems that are suspected of being infected. In some cases, non-IT staff might fulfill this duty at remote offices that do not have available IT staff. Any staff who might need to assist during major malware incidents should be designated in advance and provided with documentation and periodic training on their possible duties.

4.3.6.4 Identification Recommendations

Although active approaches typically produce the most accurate results, they are often not the fastest way of identifying infections. It might take considerable time to scan every host in an organization, and because systems that have been disconnected or shut off will not be identified, the scan will need to be repeated. If forensic data is very recent, it might be a good source of readily available information, although the information might not be comprehensive. Manual methods are generally not feasible for comprehensive enterprise-wide identification, but they are a necessary part of identification when other methods are not available, and can fill in gaps when other methods are insufficient. In many cases, it is most effective to use multiple approaches simultaneously or in sequence to provide the best results.

Organizations should carefully consider the possible approaches for their environment ahead of time, select a sufficiently broad range of approaches, and develop procedures and technical capabilities to perform each selected approach effectively when a major malware incident occurs. Organizations should also identify which individuals or groups can assist in identification efforts. For example, identification might be performed by security administrators (antivirus software, IPS, firewalls, vulnerability assessment, scans), system administrators (DNS, e-mail, and Web servers), network administrators (packet sniffers, routers), desktop administrators (Windows registry or file scans, login script changes), and others. Organizations should ensure that everyone who might be involved in identification knows what his or her role is and how to perform necessary tasks.

4.4 Eradication

Although the primary goal of eradication is to remove malware from infected systems, eradication is typically more involved than that. If an infection was successful because of a system vulnerability or other security weakness, such as an unsecured file share, then eradication includes the elimination or mitigation of that weakness, which should prevent the system from becoming reinfected or becoming infected by another instance of malware or a variant of the original threat. As mentioned in Section 4.3.6, eradication actions are often consolidated with containment efforts. For example, organizations might run a utility that identifies infected hosts, applies patches to remove vulnerabilities, and runs antivirus software that removes infections. Containment actions often limit eradication choices; for example, if an incident is contained by disconnecting infected systems from the primary network, the systems should either be connected to a separate VLAN so that they can be updated remotely, or patched and reconfigured manually. Because the hosts are disconnected from the primary network, the incident response team will be under pressure to perform eradication actions on the hosts as quickly as possible so that the users can regain full use of their systems.

Different situations necessitate various combinations of eradication techniques. The most common tools for eradication are antivirus software, spyware detection and removal utilities, and patch management software. Automated eradication methods, such as triggering antivirus scans remotely, are much more efficient than manual methods, such as visiting infected systems in person and running disinfection software from a CD, but automated methods are not the best for all situations. For example, an infected host that is attempting to cause major damage to other systems or use large amounts of bandwidth should probably stay isolated from networks and be handled through manual actions. In addition, as described in Section 4.3.1, some situations necessitate user participation in containment and eradication activities. Providing instructions and software updates to users works in some cases, but other users might need assistance. Having formal or informal walk-up help desk areas at major facilities can also be effective and is more efficient and convenient than having IT staff locate and interrupt each affected user. During major incidents, additional IT staff members can be relieved of other duties temporarily to assist in eradication efforts. For locations without IT staff, it is often helpful to have a few people trained in basic eradication actions so that they can take care of their own systems. Organizations should be prepared to perform a few different types of eradication efforts simultaneously if needed.

In some malware incidents, it may be necessary to rebuild infected hosts as part of eradication efforts. Rebuilding includes the reinstallation and securing of the OS and applications, and the restoration of data from known good backups. Because rebuilding a host is typically more resource-intensive than other eradication methods, it should be performed only when no other eradication method or combination of methods is sufficient. For example, some types of spyware are extremely difficult to remove from hosts; even if they can be removed, each host's OS may be damaged, possibly to the point where the hosts cannot boot. Rebuilding is also often the best eradication option when the actions performed on an infected host are unknown. If a host has multiple infections; has been infected for an extended or unknown period of time; or has had backdoors, rootkits, or other damaging attacker tools installed, other malicious actions besides the malware infections may have been performed against the host. In such cases, rebuilding the host would be the most reliable way of restoring its integrity. Organizations should be prepared to rebuild hosts quickly, as needed, when malware incidents occur.

Eradication can be frustrating because of the number of systems to clean up and the tendency during major incidents to have additional infections and reinfections occurring for days, weeks, or months.[41] Incident handlers should periodically perform identification activities to identify hosts that are still infected and estimate the success of the eradication. A reduction in the number of infected hosts would demonstrate that the incident response team was making progress and would help the team choose the best strategy for handling the remaining hosts and allocate sufficient time and resources. It can be tempting to declare an incident resolved once the number of infected hosts has dropped significantly from the original numbers, but the organization should strive to reduce the suspected numbers of infected and vulnerable machines to low enough levels that if they were all connected to the network at once and the vulnerable machines all became infected, the overall impact of the infections would be minimal.

Eradicating a widespread malware infection can be made even more stressful if people throughout the organization, particularly users and management, have not been previously prepared to have realistic expectations concerning how long the eradication might take. Because of the sheer number of systems involved, and the increasingly dynamic nature of systems, in many organizations it could easily take a few days or a week to perform eradication for the vast majority of infected systems, and could take weeks or months to eradicate the malware threat on virtually all systems. Performing awareness activities that set reasonable expectations for eradication and recovery efforts (as described in Section 4.5) can reduce the stress that major malware incidents can cause.

Because many rootkits make hundreds of changes to systems and their most important files, it often requires extensive time and resources to eradicate a rootkit completely from a system and verify its eradication. Typically, organizations should rebuild any system that has a rootkit or is strongly suspected of having a rootkit. Such a system should be rebuilt either by reinstalling and reconfiguring the operating system and applications, or by restoring the system from known good backups. In general, organizations should strongly consider rebuilding any system that has any of the following incident characteristics, instead of performing typical eradication actions.

■ One or more attackers gained administrator-level access to the system.

■ Unauthorized administrator-level access to the system was available to anyone through a backdoor, an unprotected share created by a worm, or other means.

■ System files were replaced by a Trojan horse, backdoor, rootkit, attacker tools, or other means.

---

[41] Instances of a particular type of malware might reside within an organization indefinitely, regardless of eradication efforts. For example, malware might be captured in system backups; restoration of a backup could also restore the malware. Also, malware might infect removable media that then sits unused for an extended period of time. Years after the initial infection, the removable media could be accessed, and the malware could attempt to infect the host. Because such threats exist on the internal network, network perimeter defenses (e.g., on the firewall) are generally not effective against them.

■ The system is unstable or does not function properly after the malware has been eradicated by antivirus software, spyware detection and removal utilities, or other programs or techniques. This indicates that either the malware has not been eradicated completely or that it has caused damage to important system or application files or settings.

If a malware incident does not have any of these characteristics, then it is typically sufficient to eradicate the malware from the system instead of rebuilding the system. When the extent of damage or unauthorized access to a system is unclear, organizations should consider rebuilding the system.

4.5 Recovery

The two main aspects of recovery from malware incidents are restoring the functionality and data of infected systems and removing temporary containment measures. Additional actions to restore systems are not necessary for most malware incidents that cause limited system damage (for example, an infection that simply altered a few data files and was completely removable with antivirus software). As discussed in Section 4.4, for malware incidents that are far more damaging, such as Trojan horses, rootkits, or backdoors, corrupting thousands of system and data files, or wiping out hard drives, it is often best to first rebuild the system or to restore it from a known good backup, then secure the system so that it is no longer vulnerable to the malware threat. Organizations should carefully consider possible worst-case scenarios, such as a new malware threat that wipes out the hard drives of a large percentage of the organization's workstations, and determine how the systems would be recovered in these cases. This should include identifying who would perform the recovery tasks, estimating how many hours of labor would be needed and how much calendar time would elapse, and determining how the recovery efforts should be prioritized.

Determining when to remove temporary containment measures, such as suspended services (e.g., e-mail) or connectivity (e.g., Internet access, VPN for telecommuters), is often a difficult decision during major malware incidents. For example, suppose that e-mail has been shut down to stop the spread of a malware infection while vulnerable systems are patched and infected systems undergo individual malware containment, eradication, and recovery measures. It might take days or weeks for all vulnerable systems to be located and patched and for all infected systems to be cleaned, but e-mail cannot remain suspended for that period of time. When e-mail service is restored, it is almost certain that an infected system will begin spreading the malware again at some time. However, if nearly all systems have been patched and cleaned, the impact of a new malware infection should be minimal. Incident response teams should strive to keep containment measures in place until the estimated number of unpatched or infected systems is sufficiently low that subsequent incidents should be of little consequence. Incident handlers should also consider alternative containment measures that could adequately maintain containment of the incident while causing less of an impact on the normal functions of the organization. However, even though the incident response team should assess the risks of restoring the service, management should ultimately be responsible for determining what should be done, based on the incident response team's recommendations and management's understanding of the business impact of maintaining the containment measures.

4.6 Lessons Learned

When a major malware incident occurs, the primary individuals performing the response usually work intensively for days or weeks. As the major handling efforts end, the key people are usually mentally and physically fatigued, and are behind in performing other tasks that were pending during the incident handling period. Consequently, the lessons learned phase of incident response might be significantly delayed or skipped altogether for major malware incidents. However, because major malware incidents can be extremely expensive to handle, it is particularly important for organizations to conduct robust lessons learned activities for major malware incidents. Although it is reasonable to give handlers and other key people a few days to catch up on other tasks, review meetings and other efforts should occur expeditiously, while the incident is still fresh in everyone's minds. The lessons learned process for malware incidents is no different than for any other type of incident. Examples of possible outcomes of lessons learned activities for malware incidents are as follows:

- **Security Policy Changes.** Security policies might be modified to prevent similar incidents. For example, if e-mail attachments ending in a *.scr* extension were used to cause a widespread infection, modifying the policy to forbid e-mailing *.scr* files might be advisable.

- **Awareness Program Changes.** Security awareness training for users might be changed to reduce the number of infections or to improve users' actions in reporting incidents and assisting with handling incidents on their own systems.

- **Software Reconfiguration.** OS or application settings might need to be changed to support security policy changes or to achieve compliance with existing policy.

- **Malware Detection Software Deployment.** If systems were infected through a transmission mechanism that was unprotected by antivirus software or other malware detection tools, an incident might provide sufficient justification to purchase and deploy additional software.

- **Malware Detection Software Reconfiguration.** Detection software might need to be reconfigured in various ways, such as the following:

  - Increasing the frequency of software and signature updates

  - Improving the accuracy of detection (e.g., fewer false positives, fewer false negatives)

  - Increasing the scope of monitoring (e.g., monitoring additional transmission mechanisms, monitoring additional files or file systems)

  - Changing the action automatically performed in response to detected malware

  - Improving the efficiency of signature update distribution.

4.7 Summary

Organizations should have a robust incident response process capability that addresses malware incident handling. As defined in NIST SP 800-61, the incident response process has four major phases: preparation, detection and analysis, containment/eradication/recovery, and post-incident activity. The following provides a summary of major recommendations for malware incident handling, listed by incident response phase:

- **Preparation.** Organizations should perform preparatory measures to ensure that they are capable of responding effectively to malware incidents. Recommended actions include the following:

  - Developing malware-specific incident handling policies and procedures that define the roles and responsibilities of all individuals and teams that might be involved in malware incident handling

  - Regularly conducting malware-oriented training and exercises

  - Building and maintaining malware-related skills for malware incident handlers, such as understanding malware infection methods and malware detection tools

- Facilitating communication and coordination by designating in advance a few individuals or a small team to be responsible for coordinating the organization's responses to malware incidents

- Establishing several communication mechanisms so that coordination among incident handlers, technical staff, management, and users can be sustained during adverse events

- Establishing a point of contact for answering questions about the legitimacy of malware alerts

- Acquiring the necessary hardware and software tools to assist in malware incident handling.

■ **Detection and Analysis.** Organizations should strive to detect and validate malware incidents rapidly, because infections can spread through an organization in a matter of minutes. Early detection can help an organization minimize the number of infected systems, which will lessen the magnitude of the recovery effort and the amount of damage the organization sustains. Recommended actions related to detection and analysis include the following:

- Monitor malware advisories and security tool alerts (e.g., antivirus software, IPSs) to detect precursors to malware incidents, which can give organizations an opportunity to prevent incidents by altering their security posture.

- Review data from the primary sources of malware incident indications, including user reports, IT staff reports, and security tools (e.g., antivirus software, IDSs), and correlate data among the sources to identify malware-related activity. Analyze suspected malware incidents and validate that malware is the cause of each incident because no indication is completely reliable. Use secondary data sources when needed to correlate activity or gather more information.

- Construct trusted toolkits on removable media that contain up-to-date tools for identifying malware, listing the currently running processes, and performing other analysis actions.

- Establish a set of prioritization criteria that identify the appropriate level of response for various types of malware-related incidents.

■ **Containment.** Containment has two major components: stopping the spread of malware and preventing further damage to systems. Nearly every malware incident requires containment actions. In addressing an incident, it is important for an organization to decide which methods of containment to employ initially, early in the response. Organizations should have strategies and procedures in place for making containment-related decisions that reflect the level of risk acceptable to the organization. The containment strategies should support incident handlers in selecting the appropriate combination of containment methods based on the characteristics of a particular situation. Organizations should support sound containment decisions by having policies that clearly state who has authority to make major containment decisions, and under what circumstances various actions are appropriate. Containment methods can be divided into four basic categories:

- **User Participation.** It can be helpful to provide users with instructions on how to identify infections and what measures to take if a system is infected can be helpful; however, organizations should not rely primarily on users for containing malware incidents.

- **Automated Detection.** Automated technologies, such as antivirus software, e-mail filtering, and intrusion prevention software, often can contain malware incidents. In a widespread incident, if malware cannot be identified by updated antivirus software, organizations should be prepared to use other security tools to contain it.

— **Disabling Services.** Organizations should be prepared to shut down or block services used by malware to contain an incident and should understand the consequences of doing so. The organization should also be prepared to respond to problems caused by other organizations disabling their own services in response to a malware incident.

— **Disabling Connectivity.** Organizations should be prepared to place additional restrictions on network connectivity to contain a malware incident, recognizing the impact that the restrictions might have on organizational functions.

Incident handlers should be familiar with the procedures for submitting copies of unknown malware to the organization's antivirus vendors and other security software vendors for analysis. Organizations should also contact trusted parties, such as incident response organizations and antivirus vendors, when needed for guidance on handling new threats.

Identifying hosts that have been infected by malware is another vital step in containing many malware incidents, particularly widespread ones. This process is often complicated by the dynamic nature of computing. Organizations should carefully consider host identification issues before a large-scale malware incident occurs so that they are prepared to use multiple strategies for identifying infected hosts as part of implementing effective containment. Organizations should then select a sufficiently broad range of identification approaches and develop procedures and technical capabilities to perform each selected approach effectively when a major malware incident occurs.

■ **Eradication.** The primary goal of eradication is to remove malware from infected systems. Because of the sheer number of systems involved, and the increasingly dynamic nature of systems, in many organizations it could easily take a few days or a week to perform eradication for the vast majority of infected systems, and weeks or months to eradicate the malware threat on virtually all systems. Organizations should be prepared to use various combinations of eradication techniques simultaneously for different situations. They also should consider performing awareness activities that set expectations for eradication and recovery efforts, which can be helpful in reducing the stress that major malware incidents can cause. If an incident has resulted in unauthorized administrator-level access or changes to system files, organizations should be prepared to rebuild each affected system either by reinstalling and reconfiguring its operating system and applications, or by restoring it from known good backups.

■ **Recovery.** The two main aspects of recovery from malware incidents are restoring the functionality and data of infected systems, and removing temporary containment measures. Organizations should carefully consider possible worst-case scenarios and determine how recovery should be performed. Determining when to remove temporary containment measures, such as suspended services or connectivity, is often a difficult decision during major malware incidents. Incident response teams should strive to keep containment measures in place until the estimated number of infected systems and systems vulnerable to infection is sufficiently low that subsequent incidents should be of little consequence. However, even though the incident response team should assess the risks of restoring services or connectivity, management should ultimately be responsible for determining what should be done, based on the incident response team's recommendations and management's understanding of the business impact of maintaining the containment measures.

■ **Post-Incident Activity.** Because malware incidents can be extremely expensive to handle, it is particularly important for organizations to conduct robust lessons learned activities for major malware incidents. Capturing the lessons following the handling of a malware incident should help an organization improve its incident handling capability and malware defenses, including needed changes to security policy, software configurations, and malware detection and prevention software deployments.

5. The Future of Malware

When planning malware prevention and malware incident handling capabilities, organizations should consider the future of malware. Because new malware threats arise constantly, organizations should establish malware prevention and handling capabilities that are robust and flexible enough to address short-term future threats and to be modified and built on to address long-term future threats. Both malware and the defenses against malware continue to evolve, each in response to improvements in the other. For most organizations, neither the malware creators nor the malware defenders are clearly prevailing at this time.

Although the future of malware threats is unknown, some expectations can reasonably be made based on the history of malware. (An overview of malware history is provided in Section 2.9.) Antivirus vendors' malware databases list dozens of new threats each week, which indicates that the frequency of new threats continues to increase. This is partially due to the ease with which variants of existing threats can be created; for example, new widespread worms often have dozens of variants released within days. Another reason for the increased frequency of new threats is the recent shift toward malicious mobile code threats, which are relatively easy to create and modify compared with some older forms of malware, such as viruses. As long as attackers do not need to be particularly skilled to change existing malware into new variants, the frequency of new threats is likely to continue to increase.

Another likely trend is an increasing number of threats that cause major damage in a very short time. The Witty worm, a network service worm released in 2004, was designed to destroy data on hard drives. According to an analysis performed by the Cooperative Association for Internet Data Analysis (CAIDA), this worm successfully infected most available targets in less than an hour from the time it began to spread on the Internet.[42] Another aspect of the Witty worm is also noteworthy: it was released a day after the vulnerability it exploited was announced publicly. This gave organizations little time to patch their systems or perform other mitigation activities before the malware was released. Attackers occasionally release an exploit even before its targeted vulnerability has been announced publicly; such threats are known as *zero-day attacks*. A zero-day attack that has the speed and destructiveness of the Witty worm and that targets a widely implemented application or OS could cause serious damage to millions of systems in a matter of minutes. It is certainly possible that such a worm could be released; organizations should consider this and think about how it could impact their operations and how they could best respond to it. Organizations should also consider deploying a combination of security controls that can detect and stop both known and unknown threats. In general, organizations should consider putting increased emphasis on security controls that are effective at stopping malicious or dangerous behavior, rather than simply detecting it.

Another major trend in malware is the increasing use of malware and other malicious content to perform fraud. Spyware, phishing attacks, and other efforts to violate privacy have been used successfully to trick users into revealing personal information, leading to many cases of identity theft and financial fraud. Current technical security controls for stopping such threats are still immature, but demand for better protection should lead to the development of much more robust spyware detection and removal utilities, as well as the addition of similar capabilities to antivirus software. As better technical controls are deployed and users become more familiar with the attackers' techniques, it seems likely that attackers will

---

[42] The analysis is explained in "The Spread of the Witty Worm", available at http://www.caida.org/analysis/security/witty/. CAIDA has also published an analysis of the Slammer worm ("The Spread of the Sapphire/Slammer Worm", located at http://www.caida.org/outreach/papers/2003/sapphire/sapphire.html); it explains that the Slammer worm infected most available vulnerable hosts within 10 minutes. Recent research suggests that worms similar to Witty and Slammer could become widespread in seconds, not minutes. See "The Top Speed of Flash Worms" (http://www.caida.org/outreach/papers/2004/topspeedworms/topspeed-worm04.pdf) for additional information.

employ more resourceful and innovative means to avoid automated detection and take advantage of the trust of users.

Attackers also have started creating viruses and worms that attack non-traditional platforms, such as PDAs and cell phones, or use them as malware carriers. As the use of mobile technologies using wireless computing continues to increase, malware incidents involving these technologies are very likely to increase in frequency and severity. This underscores the need for organizations to stay aware of the latest types of threats and the security controls available to protect against each threat type. As a new category of threats becomes more serious, organizations should plan and implement appropriate controls to mitigate them.

Appendix A—Containment Technology Summary

Various technologies that are helpful for malware incident containment are described throughout this publication. Although most of these technologies are also useful for incident prevention, detection, and eradication, this section focuses on containment because it is the most complex phase of malware incident handling. In addition, generally more technologies are relevant to the containment phase than to any other phase of malware incident handling. This appendix provides a summary of how each technology can be used for malware incident containment, and gives the reader tools for identifying which technologies are most applicable to certain situations as a basis for planning effective containment strategies.

In developing a malware incident handling strategy, organizations should consider all technologies that could be used for malware incident containment. Table A-1 lists the most commonly used technologies and provides general guidance on the effectiveness of each technology against each major category of malware and attacker tool. For the purposes of this table, environments are divided into two categories (managed and non-managed) and threats into two categories (simple and complex). The meanings of these categories are as follows:

■ **Managed Environment.** In a managed environment, one or more centralized groups have substantial control over server and workstation operating system and application configurations across the enterprise. This allows better security practices to be implemented during initial system deployment and in ongoing support and maintenance, and enables a consistent security posture to be maintained across the enterprise. The guidance in this section assumes that in managed environments, on most systems the recommended practices for malware prevention and handling are followed (e.g., installing antivirus software on all hosts and keeping it up-to-date, using default deny policies on firewalls, applying patches to operating systems and applications).

■ **Non-Managed Environment.** In a non-managed environment, system owners and users have substantial control over their own systems, typically with administrator-level privileges. Although the systems might initially use enterprise-standard configurations, owners and users can alter the configurations, which could weaken their security. The guidance in this section assumes that in non-managed environments, recommended practices for malware prevention and handling are followed on some systems, with some practices followed on most systems.

■ **Simple Threat.** A simple threat is a malware threat with a small number of identifying characteristics. For example, a mass mailing worm that uses a single fixed subject and any of three file attachment names would be considered a simple threat. Another simple threat would be a backdoor that uses one fixed port number and communicates only with one particular IP address.

■ **Complex Threat.** Unlike a simple threat, a complex threat uses any of hundreds or thousands of identifying characteristics; some complex threats even generate characteristics at random. One example is a mass mailing worm that uses any of 50 subjects and any of 50 filenames with random sender addresses, e-mail bodies, and file attachment sizes. Another example is malicious mobile code that downloads its payload from any IP address in a large list that varies among instances of the malicious mobile code. Complex threats are often more difficult to contain than simple threats.

The default guidance in Table A-1 applies to handling simple threats in managed environments.

Table A-1. Typical Effectiveness of Prevention and Containment Technologies

Technology	Simple Threat, Managed Environment	Significant Differences for Non-Managed Environment	Significant Differences for Complex Threat
Security Tools			
Network-based antivirus software	• Very effective at stopping all types of known malware that attempt to pass through monitored network points (e.g., Internet firewall); effective at stopping some unknown malware	• None	• None
Host-based antivirus software	• Very effective at stopping known malware that attempts to infect hosts (e.g., workstations, servers); effective at stopping some unknown malware	• Less effective because some hosts will have outdated, misconfigured, or disabled software, or will not have the software installed	• None
Spyware detection and removal utility (usually host-based)	• Very effective at stopping known spyware that attempts to infect hosts (e.g., workstations, servers); effective at stopping some unknown spyware	• Less effective because some hosts will have outdated, misconfigured, or disabled software, or will not have the software installed	• None
Network-based intrusion prevention system	• Effective at stopping major known worms that attempt to pass through monitored network points (e.g., Internet firewall); in certain cases, effective at stopping unknown worms • Somewhat effective at identifying and stopping use of backdoors	• None	• Generally less effective because detection accuracy is lower • If threat has random characteristics, generally not effective at all
Host-based intrusion prevention system	• Somewhat effective at stopping known and unknown malware that attempts to infect hosts (e.g., workstations, servers) • Effective at identifying malware that attempts to alter critical system files	• Less effective because some hosts will have outdated, misconfigured, or disabled software, or will not have the software installed; also, software is unlikely to be well-tuned, reducing its detection accuracy	• Generally less effective because detection accuracy is lower
Network-based spam filtering	• Very effective at stopping known e-mail-based malware that uses the organization's e-mail services; effective at stopping some unknown malware	• None	• Generally less effective because detection accuracy is lower • If threat has random characteristics, generally not effective at all
Host-based spam filtering	• Very effective at stopping known e-mail-based malware that uses the organization's e-mail services; effective at stopping some unknown malware	• Somewhat less effective because some hosts will have outdated, misconfigured, or disabled software, or will not have the software installed	• Generally less effective because detection accuracy is lower • If threat has random characteristics, generally not effective at all
Network-based Web content filtering	• Effective at stopping known Web-based malware	• None	• Generally less effective because detection accuracy is lower

Technology	Simple Threat, Managed Environment	Significant Differences for Non-Managed Environment	Significant Differences for Complex Threat
Host-based Web content filtering	• Effective at stopping known Web-based malware	• Less effective because some hosts will have outdated, misconfigured, or disabled software, or will not have the software installed	• Generally less effective because detection accuracy is lower
Network Configuration Changes			
Network-based firewall	• Very effective at preventing Internet-based worms that use network services not permitted by the firewall policy from entering or exiting networks • Effective at blocking access to external services (e.g., instant messaging) and hosts (e.g., Web sites) being used as a malware transmission mechanism • Effective at preventing e-mails generated by unauthorized hosts (e.g., workstations infected with mass mailing worms) from leaving the organization's networks • Effective at blocking access to/from attacker IP addresses by malware (e.g., backdoors, malicious mobile code, keystroke loggers, malicious browser plug-ins)	• None	• May be less effective if attempting to block access to/from many IP addresses
Host-based firewall[43]	• Very effective at preventing network service worms from infecting hosts (e.g., workstations, servers) • Effective at preventing outbound activity generated by an infected host from leaving the host (e.g., backdoors, keystroke logs, Web browser activity, e-mail generators)	• Less effective because some hosts will have outdated, misconfigured, or disabled software, or will not have the software installed	• None
Internet border router	• Very effective at preventing entry to the organization's network by Internet-based worms that use network services not permitted by the perimeter security policy • Effective at blocking access to/from attacker IP addresses by malware (e.g., backdoors, malicious mobile code, keystroke loggers, malicious browser plug-ins)	• None	• May be less effective if attempting to block access to/from many IP addresses

---

43   This item includes only the firewalling capabilities of a host-based firewall product, not other capabilities that the product might include, such as antivirus software, host-based intrusion prevention, spam filtering, or Web content filtering.

Technology	Simple Threat, Managed Environment	Significant Differences for Non-Managed Environment	Significant Differences for Complex Threat
Internal router	• Very effective at preventing worms that use network services not permitted by the firewall policy from entering or exiting the organization's network and subnets • Effective at blocking access to/from attacker IP addresses by malware (e.g., backdoors, malicious mobile code, keystroke loggers, malicious browser plug-ins) • Somewhat effective at blocking outbound e-mail activity generated by e-mail generators on infected hosts	• None	• May be less effective if attempting to block access to/from many IP addresses
Host Configuration Changes			
Host hardening (including patching)	• Effective at stopping additional infections for instances of malware that exploit vulnerabilities or insecure settings	• Less effective because more hosts will not be patched or hardened quickly or properly	• None
E-mail server settings (e.g., blocking e-mail attachments)	• Very effective at stopping e-mail-based malware that uses the organization's e-mail services	• None	• Generally less effective because detection accuracy is lower • If threat has random characteristics, generally not effective at all
Settings for other services housed on the organization's servers	• Somewhat effective to very effective at stopping network service worms	• None	• Generally less effective because detection accuracy is lower • If threat has random characteristics, generally not effective at all
Application client settings (e.g., limiting mobile code execution for e-mail clients or Web browsers, restricting macro use in word processors)	• Effective at stopping some specific instances of malware	• Limited effectiveness, because users need to perform an action to implement the settings (e.g., change settings manually, run a distributed tool or script)	• None

Tables A-2 and A-3 summarize the information from Table A-1, indicating each technology's effectiveness against simple (Table A-2) and complex (Table A-3) threats in managed environments. These tables provide separate ratings for how well each technology typically handles each type of malware, as well as each attacker tool type. Ratings are as follows: H = high effectiveness against threat category; M = moderate effectiveness; L = low effectiveness. Typically, a rating of moderate or low effectiveness means that the technology works well for certain cases but poorly or not at all for other cases. A blank cell indicates the technology generally does not apply to the given threat. Tables A-4 and A-5 provide assessments of technologies' effectiveness against simple (Table A-4) and complex (Table A-5) threats in non-managed environments.

Table A-2. Typical Effectiveness Against Simple Threats in Managed Environments

Technologies	Multipartite Virus	Macro Virus	Network Service Worm	Mass Mailing Worm	Trojan Horse	Malicious Mobile Code	Backdoor[44]	Keystroke Logger	Rootkit	Malicious Browser Plug-ins	E-mail Generators
Security Tools											
Network-based antivirus software	H	H	H	H	H	H	H	H	H	H	H
Host-based antivirus software	H	H	H	H	H	H	H	H	H	H	H
Spyware detection and removal utility					H	H				H	
Network-based intrusion prevention system			M	M			L				
Host-based intrusion prevention system			L		M	L	L	L	M	L	L
Network-based spam filtering				H	L	M					H
Host-based spam filtering				H	L	M					H
Network-based Web content filtering					L	M				M	
Host-based Web content filtering					L	M				M	
Network Configuration Changes											
Network-based firewall			H	M	M	M	M	M		M	M
Host-based firewall			H	H	M	M	M	M		M	M
Internet border router			H			M	M	M		M	
Internal router			H		L	M	M	M		M	L
Host Configuration Changes											
Host hardening (including patching)	L	L	M	M	M	M					
E-mail server settings (e.g., blocking e-mail attachments)	L	L		H	M	M					H
Settings for other services housed on the organization's servers			L-H								
Application client settings (e.g., limiting mobile code execution for e-mail clients or Web browsers, restricting macro use in word processors)		M	M			M				M	

---

44 This category includes bots and remote administration tools.

Table A-3. Typical Effectiveness Against Complex Threats in Managed Environments

Technologies	Malware Type						Attacker Tool Type				
	Multipartite Virus	Macro Virus	Network Service Worm	Mass Mailing Worm	Trojan Horse	Malicious Mobile Code	Backdoor	Keystroke Logger	Rootkit	Malicious Browser Plug-Ins	E-mail Generators
Security Tools											
Network-based antivirus software	H	H	H	H	H	H	H	H	H	H	H
Host-based antivirus software	H	H	H	H	H	H	H	H	H	H	H
Spyware detection and removal utility					H	H				H	
Network-based intrusion prevention system			L	L	L	L	L	L	L		L
Host-based intrusion prevention system			L		L	L	L	L	L	L	
Network-based spam filtering				L-M	L	L					L-M
Host-based spam filtering				L-M	L	L					L-M
Network-based Web content filtering					L	L				L	
Host-based Web content filtering					L	L				L	
Network Configuration Changes											
Network-based firewall			H	M	M	M	L-M	L-M		L-M	L-M
Host-based firewall			H		L	M	M	M		M	M
Internet border router			H			M	L-M	L-M		L-M	
Internal router			H			M	L-M	L-M		L-M	L
Host Configuration Changes											
Host hardening (including patching)	L	L	M	M	M	M					
E-mail server settings (e.g., blocking e-mail attachments)	L	L		L-M	L	L					L-M
Settings for other services housed on the organization's servers			L-M								
Application client settings (e.g., limiting mobile code execution for e-mail clients or Web browsers, restricting macro use in word processors)		M				M				M	

Table A-4. Typical Effectiveness Against Simple Threats in Non-Managed Environments

Technologies	Malware Type						Attacker Tool Type				
	Multipartite Virus	Macro Virus	Network Service Worm	Mass Mailing Worm	Trojan Horse	Malicious Mobile Code	Backdoor	Keystroke Logger	Rootkit	Malicious Browser Plug-ins	E-mail Generators
Security Tools											
Network-based antivirus software	H	H	H	H	H	H	H	H	H	H	H
Host-based antivirus software	M	M	M	M	M	M	M	M	M	M	M
Spyware detection and removal utility			M	M	M	M				M	
Network-based intrusion prevention system			M			L	L				
Host-based intrusion prevention system			L		L	L	L	L	L	L	L
Network-based spam filtering				H	L	M					H
Host-based spam filtering				M	L	M					M
Network-based Web content filtering					L	M				M	
Host-based Web content filtering					L	M				M	
Network Configuration Changes											
Network-based firewall			H	M		M	M	M		M	M
Host-based firewall			M			M	M	M		M	M
Internet border router			H			M	M	M		M	M
Internal router			H			M	M	M		M	L
Host Configuration Changes											
Host hardening (including patching)	L	L	L–M	L–M	L–M	L–M					
E-mail server settings (e.g., blocking e-mail attachments)	L	L		H	M	M					H
Settings for other services housed on the organization's servers			L–H								
Application client settings (e.g., limiting mobile code execution for e-mail clients or Web browsers, restricting macro use in word processors)		L	L			L				L	

Table A-5. Typical Effectiveness Against Complex Threats in Non-Managed Environments

Technologies	Malware Type						Attacker Tool Type				
	Multipartite Virus	Macro Virus	Network Service Worm	Mass Mailing Worm	Trojan Horse	Malicious Mobile Code	Backdoor	Keystroke Logger	Rootkit	Malicious Browser Plug-Ins	E-mail Generators
Security Tools											
Network-based antivirus software	H	H	H	H	H	H	H	H	H	H	H
Host-based antivirus software	M	M	M	M	M	M	M	M	M	M	M
Spyware detection and removal utility					M	M	L			M	
Network-based intrusion prevention system			L	L	L	L	L	L	L	L	L
Host-based intrusion prevention system			L		L	L	L	L	L	L	
Network-based spam filtering				L–M							L–M
Host-based spam filtering				L–M							L–M
Network-based Web content filtering					L	L				L	
Host-based Web content filtering					L	L				L	
Network Configuration Changes											
Network-based firewall			H	M	L–M	M	L–M	L–M		L–M	L–M
Host-based firewall			M		L	M	M	M		M	M
Internet border router			H			M	L–M	L–M		L–M	
Internal router			H			M	L–M	L–M		L–M	L
Host Configuration Changes											
Host hardening (including patching)	L	L	L–M	L–M	L–M	L–M					
E-mail server settings (e.g., blocking e-mail attachments)	L	L		L–M	L	L					L–M
Settings for other services housed on the organization's servers			L–M								
Application client settings (e.g., limiting mobile code execution for e-mail clients or Web browsers, restricting macro use in word processors)		L				L				L	

When organizations develop strategies for malware incident containment, they should consider developing tools to assist incident handlers in selecting and implementing containment strategies quickly when a serious incident occurs. For example, suppose that a new network service worm attacks an organization and appears to be exploiting a vulnerability in the organization's host-based firewall software. The worm has relatively simple characteristics, and the organization has a great degree of centralized control over hosts' operating systems and applications, so the organization's containment strategy should be based on Table A-2. One possible strategy would be to contact the administrators of all high-effectiveness technologies first, in the most suitable sequence, which in this case could comprise the following:

1. Network and host-based antivirus software[45]

   ■ Detect and stop the worm

   ■ Identify and clean infected systems

2. Host-based firewalls

   ■ Block worm activity from entering or exiting hosts

   ■ Reconfigure the host-based firewall software itself to prevent exploitation by the worm

   ■ Update the host-based firewall software so that it is no longer exploitable

3. Network firewalls

   ■ Detect and stop the worm from entering or exiting networks and subnets

4. Internet border and internal routers

   ■ Detect and stop the worm from entering or exiting networks and subnets if the volume of traffic is too high for network firewalls to handle or if certain subnets need greater protection

At the incident handlers' discretion, they could also contact the administrators of other technologies, such as network-based and host-based intrusion prevention systems, to determine whether they could configure their systems to stop the worm.

---

[45] If the host-based firewall does not use an application protocol that is monitored and analyzed by the network antivirus software, then the network antivirus software might not be helpful in this case.

In a non-managed environment, it is unlikely that host-based firewalls would be centrally controlled. Accordingly, incident handlers could not rely on the host-based firewalls being updated, reconfigured, or otherwise modified to assist in containment. Incident handlers would therefore have to rely much more heavily on network-based controls for containment, such as network firewalls and routers, and would not be able to perform incident handling at the host level.

Appendix B—Malware Incident Handling Scenarios

Exercises involving malware incident handling scenarios provide an inexpensive and effective way to build incident response skills and identify potential issues with malware incident response processes. In these exercises, persons who participate in the malware incident responses are presented with a brief malware scenario and a list of related questions. The group then discusses each question and determines the most likely answer. The goal is to determine what the responders would really do if the scenario were to occur in real life and to compare that response with policies, procedures, and generally recommended practices to identify any discrepancies or deficiencies. For example, the answer to one question might indicate that the response would be delayed because the incident response team lacked a particular piece of software or because another team within the organization did not provide off-hours support.

The questions listed in Section B.1 are applicable to almost any malware scenario. These questions are followed by several specific scenarios, each of which is followed by additional scenario-specific questions. Organizations are strongly encouraged to adapt these questions and scenarios for use in their own incident response exercises.

B.1 Scenario Questions

Preparation/Prevention:

1. What measures are in place to attempt to prevent this type of malware incident from occurring or to limit its impact?

Detection and Analysis:

1. What precursors of the malware incident, if any, might the organization detect? Would any precursors cause the organization to attempt to take action before the incident occurred?

2. What indications of the malware incident might the organization detect? Which indications would cause someone to think that a malware incident might have occurred?

3. How would the incident response team analyze and validate this incident?

4. To which people and groups within the organization would the team report the incident?

5. How would the incident response team prioritize the handling of this incident?

Containment, Eradication, and Recovery:

1. What strategy should the organization take to contain the incident? Why is this strategy preferable to others?

2. What could happen if the incident were not contained?

Post-Incident Activity:

1. Who would attend the lessons learned meeting regarding this incident?

2. What could be done to prevent similar incidents from occurring in the future?

3. What could be done to improve detection of similar incidents?

General Questions:

1. How many incident response team members would participate in handling this incident?

2. Besides the incident response team, what groups or individuals within the organization would be involved in handling this incident?

3. To which external parties would the team report the incident? When would each report occur? How would each report be made?

4. What other communications with external parties might occur?

5. What tools and resources would the team use in handling this incident?

6. What aspects of the handling would have been different if the incident had occurred at a different day and time (on-hours versus off-hours)?

7. What aspects of the handling would have been different if the incident had occurred at a different physical location (onsite versus offsite)?

B.2 Scenarios

Scenario 1: Worm and DDoS Agent Infestation

On a Tuesday morning, a new worm is released on the Internet. The worm exploits a Microsoft Windows vulnerability that was publicly announced 2 weeks before, at which time patches were released. The worm spreads itself through two methods: (1) e-mailing itself to all addresses that it can locate on an infected host and (2) identifying and sending itself to hosts with open Windows shares. The worm is designed to generate a different attachment name for each copy that it mails; each attachment has a randomly generated filename that uses one of over a dozen file extensions. The worm also chooses from more than 100 e-mail subjects and a similar number of e-mail bodies. When the worm infects a host, it gains administrative rights and attempts to download a distributed denial of service (DDoS) agent from different Internet Protocol (IP) addresses using File Transfer Protocol (FTP). (The number of IP addresses providing the agent is unknown.) Although the antivirus vendors quickly post warnings about the worm, it spreads very rapidly, before any of the vendors have released signatures. The organization has already incurred widespread infections before antivirus signatures become available 3 hours after the worm started to spread.

The following are additional questions for this scenario:

1. How would the incident response team identify all infected hosts?

2. How would the organization attempt to prevent the worm from entering the organization before antivirus signatures were released?

3. How would the organization attempt to prevent the worm from being spread by infected hosts before antivirus signatures were released?

4. Would the organization attempt to patch all vulnerable machines? If so, how would this be done?

5. How would the handling of this incident change if infected hosts that had received the DDoS agent had been configured to attack another organization's Web site the next morning?

6. How would the incident response team keep the organization's users informed about the status of the incident? What if e-mail services were overloaded or unavailable due to the worm?

7. What additional measures, if any, would the team use to take care of hosts that were not currently connected to the network (e.g., staff members on vacation, offsite employees who dial in occasionally)?

Scenario 2: Outbound DDoS Attack

On a Sunday night, one of the organization's network intrusion detection sensors alerts on suspected outbound DDoS activity involving a high volume of Internet Control Message Protocol (ICMP) pings. The intrusion analyst reviews the alerts; although the analyst cannot confirm that the alerts are accurate, they do not match any known false positives. The analyst contacts the incident response team so that it can investigate the activity further. Because the DDoS activity uses spoofed source IP addresses, it takes considerable time and effort to determine which host or hosts within the organization are producing it; meanwhile, the DDoS activity continues. The investigation shows that seven servers appear to be generating the DDoS traffic. Initial analysis of the servers shows that each contains signs of a DDoS rootkit.

The following are additional questions for this scenario:

1. How would the team determine which hosts within the organization were producing the traffic? Which other teams might assist the incident response team?

2. After identifying a server that was producing the traffic, how would the team determine whether the server was infected with malware?

Scenario 3: Unauthorized Access to Payroll Records

On a Wednesday evening, the organization's physical security team receives a call from a payroll administrator who caught an unknown person leaving her office. The administrator saw the person run down the hallway and enter a staircase that leads to a building exit. The administrator had left her workstation unlocked and unattended for only a few minutes. The payroll program is still logged in and on the main menu screen, as it had been when the administrator left it, but she notices that the mouse appears to have been moved. The incident response team has been asked to acquire evidence related to the incident and to determine what actions were performed (e.g., payroll data access or modification, Trojan horse delivery).

The following are additional questions for this scenario:

1. How would the team determine what actions had been performed and what malware (if any) had been installed?

2. Because of the known intruder, how would the handling of this incident differ from other malware-related incidents?

Scenario 4: Telecommuting Compromise

On a Saturday night, network intrusion detection software records some probes and scans originating from an internal IP address. Host intrusion detection software on a few servers also records some of the probes and scans. The intrusion detection analyst determines that the internal IP address belongs to the organization's virtual private networking (VPN) server and contacts the incident response team. The team reviews the intrusion detection, firewall, and VPN server logs and identifies the external IP address that is generating the activity, the user ID that was authenticated for the session, and the name of the user associated with the user ID.

The following are additional questions for this scenario:

1. Suppose that the identified user's personal computer had become compromised by a game containing a Trojan horse that was downloaded by a family member. How would this affect the handling of the incident?

2. Suppose that the identified user's personal computer had become compromised by a network service worm. How would this affect the handling of the incident?

Scenario 5: Application Crashes

On a Monday morning, the organization's help desk receives calls from three users who are having problems with their spreadsheet applications crashing repeatedly during use. As the day progresses, additional users call with similar problems. Most of the users are on the same team or related teams.

1. What types of malware could be causing the spreadsheet application crashes? What are the most likely non-malware causes?

2. What steps should be taken to determine if the crashes are caused by malware?

Scenario 6: Malicious Mobile Code

On a Friday afternoon, several users contact the help desk to report strange popup windows and toolbars in their Web browsers. The users' descriptions of the behavior are similar, so the help desk agents believe that the users' systems have been affected by the same thing, and that the most likely cause is Web-based malicious mobile code.

1. How would the incident response team determine what vulnerability or configuration settings permitted the malicious mobile code to infect the systems?

2. How would the incident response team determine what Web site or sites sent the malicious mobile code to the users' systems?

Scenario 7: Blended Malware Attack

Shortly after the organization adopts a new instant messaging platform, its users are hit with a widespread malware attack that propagates itself through the use of instant messaging. Based on the initial reports from security administrators, the attack appears to be caused by a worm. However, subsequent reports indicate that the attacks also involve Web servers and Web clients. The instant messaging and Web-based attacks appear to be related to the worm because they display the same message to users.

1. Since the malware is most likely a blended attack, how would the response differ from that for a worm?

2. Which attack vector would the organization focus its containment measures on first, and why?

Appendix C—Glossary

Selected terms used in the *Guide to Malware Incident Prevention and Handling* are defined below.

Antivirus Software: A program that monitors a computer or network to identify all major types of malware and prevent or contain malware incidents.

Backdoor: A malicious program that listens for commands on a certain Transmission Control Protocol (TCP) or User Datagram Protocol (UDP) port.

Blended Attack: An instance of malware that uses multiple infection or transmission methods.

Boot Sector Virus: A virus that infects the master boot record (MBR) of a hard drive or the boot sector of removable media, such as floppy diskettes.

Compiled Viruses: A virus that has had its source code converted by a compiler program into a format that can be directly executed by an operating system.

Cookie: A small data file that holds information regarding the use of a particular Web site.

Deny by Default: A configuration for a firewall or router that denies all incoming and outgoing traffic that is not expressly permitted, such as unnecessary services that could be used to spread malware.

Disinfecting: Removing malware from within a file.

Egress Filtering: Blocking outgoing packets that should not exit a network.

False Negative: An instance in which a security tool intended to detect a particular threat fails to do so.

False Positive: An instance in which a security tool incorrectly classifies benign content as malicious.

File Infector Virus: A virus that attaches itself to executable programs, such as word processors, spreadsheet applications, and computer games.

Host-Based Intrusion Prevention System: A program that monitors the characteristics of a single host and the events occurring within the host to identify and stop suspicious activity.

Indication: A sign that a malware incident may have occurred or may be occurring.

Ingress Filtering: Blocking incoming packets that should not enter a network.

Interpreted Virus: A virus that is composed of source code that can be executed only by a particular application or service.

Keystroke Logger: A device that monitors and records keyboard usage.

Macro Virus: A virus that attaches itself to application documents, such as word processing files and spreadsheets, and uses the application's macro programming language to execute and propagate.

Malicious Code: See "Malware".

Malware: A program that is inserted into a system, usually covertly, with the intent of compromising the confidentiality, integrity, or availability of the victim's data, applications, or operating system or of otherwise annoying or disrupting the victim.

Mass Mailing Worm: A worm that spreads by identifying e-mail addresses, often by searching an infected system, and then sending copies of itself to those addresses, either using the system's e-mail client or a self-contained mailer built into the worm itself.

Memory Resident: A virus that stays in the memory of infected systems for an extended period of time.

Mobile Code: Software that is transmitted from a remote system to be executed on a local system, typically without the user's explicit instruction.

Multipartite Virus: A virus that uses multiple infection methods, typically infecting both files and boot sectors.

Network Service Worm: A worm that spreads by taking advantage of a vulnerability in a network service associated with an operating system or an application.

Network-Based Intrusion Prevention System: A program that performs packet sniffing and analyzes network traffic to identify and stop suspicious activity.

Obfuscation Technique: A way of constructing a virus to make it more difficult to detect.

On-Access Scanning: Configuring a security tool to perform real-time scans of each file for malware as the file is downloaded, opened, or executed.

On-Demand Scanning: Allowing users to launch security tool scans for malware on a computer as desired.

Payload: The portion of a virus that contains the code for the virus's objective, which may range from the relatively benign (e.g., annoying people, stating personal opinions) to the highly malicious (e.g., forwarding personal information to others, wiping out systems).

Persistent Cookie: A cookie stored on a computer indefinitely so that a Web site can identify the user during subsequent visits.

Phishing: Tricking individuals into disclosing sensitive personal information through deceptive computer-based means.

Precursor: A sign that a malware attack may occur in the future.

Proxy: A program that receives a request from a client, and then sends a request on the client's behalf to the desired destination.

Quarantining: Storing files containing malware in isolation for future disinfection or examination.

Remote Administration Tool: A program installed on a system that allows remote attackers to gain access to the system as needed.

Rootkit: A collection of files that is installed on a system to alter the standard functionality of the system in a malicious and stealthy way.

Session Cookie: A temporary cookie that is valid only for a single Web site session.

Signature: A set of characteristics of known malware instances that can be used to identify known malware and some new variants of known malware.

Spyware: Malware intended to violate a user's privacy.

Spyware Detection and Removal Utility: A program that monitors a computer to identify spyware and prevent or contain spyware incidents.

Tracking Cookie: A cookie placed on a user's computer to track the user's activity on different Web sites, creating a detailed profile of the user's behavior.

Trigger: A condition that causes a virus payload to be executed, usually occurring through user interaction (e.g., opening a file, running a program, clicking on an e-mail file attachment).

Trojan Horse: A non-replicating program that appears to be benign but actually has a hidden malicious purpose.

Virus: A form of malware that is designed to self-replicate—make copies of itself—and distribute the copies to other files, programs, or computers.

Web Browser Plug-In: A mechanism for displaying or executing certain types of content through a Web browser.

Web Bug: A tiny graphic on a Web site that is referenced within the Hypertext Markup Language (HTML) content of a Web page or e-mail to collect information about the user viewing the HTML content.

Worm: A self-replicating program that is completely self-contained and self-propagating.

Zombie: A program that is installed on a system to cause it to attack other systems.

Appendix D—Acronyms

Selected acronyms used in the *Guide to Malware Incident Prevention and Handling* are defined below.

ACL	Access Control List
APWG	Anti-Phishing Working Group
ASC	Anti-Spyware Coalition
AVIEN	Anti-Virus Information Exchange Network
BIOS	Basic Input/Output System
CAIDA	Cooperative Association for Internet Data Analysis
CARO	Computer Antivirus Research Organization
CD	Compact Disc
CIAC	Computer Incident Advisory Capability
CME	Common Malware Enumeration
CSRC	Computer Security Resource Center
DDoS	Distributed Denial of Service
DNS	Domain Name System
DShield	Distributed Intrusion Detection System
DVD	Digital Video Disc
EICAR	European Institute for Computer Antivirus Research
FAQ	Frequently Asked Questions
FISMA	Federal Information Security Management Act
FTC	Federal Trade Commission
FTP	File Transfer Protocol
HTML	Hypertext Markup Language
HTTP	Hypertext Transfer Protocol
ICMP	Internet Control Message Protocol
ID	Identification
IDS	Intrusion Detection System
IETF	Internet Engineering Task Force
IIS	Internet Information Services
IP	Internet Protocol
IPS	Intrusion Prevention System
ISC	Internet Storm Center
IT	Information Technology
ITL	Information Technology Laboratory
MAC	Media Access Control
MBR	Master Boot Record
NAP	Network Access Protection
NAT	Network Address Translation
NIST	National Institute of Standards and Technology
NSRL	National Software Reference Library

OMB	Office of Management and Budget
OS	Operating System
PDA	Personal Digital Assistant
PIN	Personal Identification Number
RAT	Remote Administration Tool
RFC	Request for Comment
SI	System and Information Integrity
SMTP	Simple Mail Transfer Protocol
SP	Special Publication
TCP	Transmission Control Protocol
UDP	User Datagram Protocol
USB	Universal Serial Bus
US-CERT	United States Computer Emergency Readiness Team
VBScript	Visual Basic Script
VLAN	Virtual Local Area Network
VPN	Virtual Private Network

Appendix E—Print Resources

Erbschloe, Michael. *Trojans, Worms, and Spyware: A Computer Security Professional's Guide to Malicious Code*. Butterworth-Heinemann, 2004.

Feinstein, Ken. *How to Do Everything to Fight Spam, Viruses, Pop-Ups, and Spyware*. McGraw-Hill Osborne Media, 2004.

Grimes, Roger. *Malicious Mobile Code: Virus Protection for Windows*. O'Reilly, 2001.

McClure, Stuart, et al. *Hacking Exposed: Network Security Secrets & Solutions, Fifth Edition*. McGraw-Hill Osborne Media, 2005.

Nazario, Jose. *Defense and Detection Strategies Against Internet Worms*. Artech House Publishers, 2003.

Prosise, Chris, et al. *Incident Response and Computer Forensics, Second Edition*. McGraw-Hill Osborne Media, 2003.

Schweitzer, Douglas. *Securing the Network from Malicious Code: A Complete Guide to Defending Against Viruses, Worms, and Trojans*. Wiley, 2002.

Skoudis, Ed, and Lenny Zeltser. *Malware: Fighting Malicious Code*. Prentice Hall PTR, 2003.

Szor, Peter. *The Art of Computer Virus Research and Defense*. Addison-Wesley, 2005.

Tittel, Ed. *PC Magazine Fighting Spyware, Viruses, and Malware*. John Wiley & Sons, 2004.

Virus Bulletin (magazine). Virus Bulletin Ltd.

Appendix F—Online Resources

The following lists provide examples of online resources that may be helpful in understanding malware and in preventing and handling malware incidents.

Organizations

Organization	URL
Anti-Phishing Working Group (APWG)	http://www.antiphishing.org/
Anti-Spyware Coalition (ASC)	http://www.antispywarecoalition.org/
Anti-Virus Information Exchange Network (AVIEN)	http://www.avien.org/
Common Malware Enumeration (CME)	http://cme.mitre.org/
Computer Antivirus Research Organization (CARO)	http://www.caro.org/
Computer Incident Advisory Capability (CIAC)	http://www.ciac.org/ciac/
Cooperative Association for Internet Data Analysis (CAIDA)	http://www.caida.org/
Distributed Intrusion Detection System (DShield)	http://dshield.org/
European Institute for Computer Antivirus Research (EICAR)	http://www.eicar.org/
Internet Storm Center (ISC)	http://isc.incidents.org/
SANS Institute	http://www.sans.org/
United States Computer Emergency Readiness Team (US-CERT)	http://www.us-cert.gov/
Virus Bulletin	http://www.virusbtn.com/
Viruslist.com	http://www.viruslist.com/en/
WildList Organization International	http://www.wildlist.org/

Technical Resource Sites

Resource Name	URL
C|Net Download.com—Spyware Center	http://www.download.com/Spyware-Center/2001-2023_4-0.html?tag=dir
Computer Associates Virus Information Center	http://www3.ca.com/securityadvisor/virusinfo/default.aspx
CSRC—Practices & Checklist/Implementation Guides	http://csrc.nist.gov/pcig/cig.html
F-Secure Security Information Center	http://www.f-secure.com/virus-info/
McAfee AVERT Virus Information Library	http://vil.nai.com/vil/default.asp
SANS Malware FAQ	http://www.sans.org/resources/malwarefaq/
SecurityFocus Virus	http://www.securityfocus.com/virus/
Sophos Virus Analyses	http://www.sophos.com/virusinfo/analyses/
Spywaredata.com	http://www.spywaredata.com/
Symantec Security Response—Search and Latest Virus Threats Page	http://securityresponse.symantec.com/avcenter/vinfodb.html
Trend Micro Virus Encyclopedia Search	http://www.trendmicro.com/vinfo/virusencyclo/
Unassigned IP Address Ranges	http://www.cymru.com/Documents/bogon-list.html
Vmyths.com—Truth About Computer Virus Myths & Hoaxes	http://www.vmyths.com/

Mailing Lists and Notification Services

Mailing List/Notification Service Name	Location
Focus-Virus	http://www.securityfocus.com/archive/100/
F-Secure Radar	http://www.f-secure.com/products/radar/
Incidents	http://www.securityfocus.com/archive/75/
McAfee AVERT Alerts	http://vil.nai.com/vil/content/alert.htm
Sophos Email Notification	http://www.sophos.com/virusinfo/notifications/
Symantec Security Response—Alerting Offerings	http://securityresponse.symantec.com/avcenter/alerting_offerings.html
Trend Micro Newsletters	http://www.trendmicro.com/subscriptions/default.asp

Other Technical Resource Documents

Resource Name	URL
CAIDA, *The Spread of the Sapphire/Slammer Worm*	http://www.caida.org/outreach/papers/2003/sapphire/sapphire.html
CAIDA, *The Spread of the Witty Worm*	http://www.caida.org/analysis/security/witty/
CAIDA, *The Top Speed of Flash Worms*	http://www.caida.org/outreach/papers/2004/topspeedworms/topspeed-worm04.pdf
CARO, CARO Virus Naming Convention	http://www.caro.org/tiki-index.php?page=CaroNamingScheme
FTC, *How Not to Get Hooked by a "Phishing" Scam*	http://ftc.gov/bcp/conline/pubs/alerts/phishingalrt.htm
IETF, RFC 2267, *Network Ingress Filtering: Defeating Denial of Service Attacks Which Employ IP Source Address Spoofing*	http://www.ietf.org/rfc/rfc2267.txt
Infoplease, Computer Virus Timeline	http://www.infoplease.com/ipa/A0872842.html
Microsoft, *The Antivirus Defense-in-Depth Guide*	http://www.microsoft.com/technet/security/topics/serversecurity/avdind_0.mspx
NIST, SP 800-28, *Guidelines on Active Content and Mobile Code*	http://csrc.nist.gov/publications/nistpubs/index.html
NIST, SP 800-31, *Intrusion Detection Systems*	http://csrc.nist.gov/publications/nistpubs/index.html
NIST, SP 800-40, *Creating a Patch and Vulnerability Management Program*	http://csrc.nist.gov/publications/nistpubs/index.html
NIST, SP 800-42, *Guideline on Network Security Testing*	http://csrc.nist.gov/publications/nistpubs/index.html
NIST, SP 800-45, *Guidelines on Electronic Mail Security*	http://csrc.nist.gov/publications/nistpubs/index.html
NIST, SP 800-53, *Recommended Security Controls for Federal Information Systems*	http://csrc.nist.gov/publications/nistpubs/index.html
NIST, SP 800-61, *Computer Security Incident Handling Guide*	http://csrc.nist.gov/publications/nistpubs/index.html
NIST, SP 800-70, *Security Configuration Checklists Program for IT Products*	http://csrc.nist.gov/checklists/
NIST, SP 800-86 (DRAFT), *Guide to Applying Forensic Techniques to Incident Response*	http://csrc.nist.gov/publications/nistpubs/index.html
NIST, *Threat Assessment of Malicious Code and Human Threats*	http://csrc.nist.gov/publications/nistir/threats/threats.html
Washington Post, *A Short History of Computer Viruses and Attacks*	http://www.washingtonpost.com/ac2/wp-dyn/A50636-2002Jun26?start=15&per=18

Z